Mastering
THE BUSINESS OF
Remodeling

An *Action Plan* for Profit,
Progress and Peace of Mind

■

Linda W. Case
Victoria L. Downing

■

Remodeling Consulting Services, Inc.
Silver Spring, Maryland

Mastering
THE BUSINESS OF
Remodeling

An *Action Plan* for Profit, Progress and Peace of Mind

■

Also By Linda Case and Victoria Downing

The Remodeler's Guide to Making and Managing Money

The Remodeler's Marketing PowerPak

Selling Remodeling: Nine Steps to Sales Success

Design Build for Remodelers, Custom Builders and Architects

Mastering
THE BUSINESS OF
Remodeling
An *Action Plan* for Profit,
Progress and Peace of Mind

By Linda W. Case and Victoria L. Downing

Published by:

■   □   ■
REMODELING
CONSULTING
SERVICES
INCORPORATED

Remodeling Consulting Services, Inc.
9834 Capitol View Avenue
Silver Spring, MD 20910 U.S.A.

Copyright © 1997 by Linda W. Case, Victoria L. Downing
First Printing 1997

Printed in the United States of America.
Library of Congress Catalog Card Number 97-69352
ISBN: 0-9648587-5-4

Cover & book design by Cristina Diez de Medina, A Scribbler's Press.

Index

FOREWORD

While you might read this book a year or two after it is written, it is a direct communication between us. We want to make your business life easier, more balanced and definitely more profitable. We've tried to write a friendly book that makes learning pleasant. We've mixed the basic and the state-of-the-art by including two special features: **Coaching Tips** which highlights our learnings as business management consultants, and **Voices of Experience** which adds the wisdom of practicing businesspeople and remodelers.

How do we know of what we write? We know because of the generosity of you and your peers. Hundreds of remodelers each year come to us for help with profitability, personnel, growth issues, diversification, marketing and sales. From these clients we've learned what works and what doesn't.

Who did we write this book for? It's directed at remodelers large and small who want to develop self-correcting systems in their companies that will grow as they do. It's for remodelers who want to glean every bit of knowledge and skill from books, tapes, their peers and their employees and put that knowledge to work in this tough business. It's for remodelers who want to change for the better before change is thrust upon them.

It's our pleasure to make this journey with you.

Linda Case and Victoria Downing

1

Seven Critical Challenges

The person who relishes challenges will be well served by this business. Remodeling is full of challenges—large and small. But remodelers are experienced problem solvers and challenges don't represent a threat—they represent an opportunity. Those remodelers who fail focus on the wrong challenges. They haven't looked at the big picture. If they had, they would have seen that the most important challenges aren't on the jobsite—they exist in the remodeler's mind and how that mind shapes and organizes the business.

Your success or failure as a remodeler will result from how well you meet and solve these seven critical challenges—

◄ The Vision Challenge

◄ The Growth Challenge

◄ The Pricing Challenge

◄ The Marketing Challenge

◄ The Employee Challenge

◄ The Quality Challenge

◄ The Customer Service Challenge

The Vision Challenge. Do you have a clear and simple idea of what your business should be—a Vision against which all other ideas and actions can be tested? Will you be able to communicate this vision to all your employees so that they share it and invest in it? In Chapter 2, we address your role as leader in your company as well as your role as worker.

The Growth Challenge. Many remodeling companies have "succeeded their way to failure." Uncontrolled growth is a business killer. When sales outstrip the delivery system, quality suffers. Customers and employees desert the company. Set a realistic limit on growth so commitments to customers and to employees are met. Many of today's booming economic areas will push remodeling companies to expand beyond their capabilities if the owners are not disciplined about growth. In Chapter 3 we focus on the development of your business including how remodeling companies are organized at each volume level. We address some varied approaches to successful growth.

The Pricing Challenge. The remodeling industry is plagued with amateurs stealing work from professionals. Thus, no professional remodeling company can be the least expensive. A carpenter working for wages will always price a job more cheaply. Therefore you as a professional remodeler must learn to market and sell the value and quality you offer in order to support the markup that is necessary to thrive in this industry. This is a difficult riddle that every professional must solve. You solve this riddle with first class marketing that brings in value-oriented leads (Chapters 7,8 and 9), with professional selling that stresses the benefits and consistency that will entice your buyer to pay a professional's price (Chapters 10 and 11), and with excellence in delivery through well-organized production systems (Chapters 12,13 and 14) manned by skilled craftsman who are also excellent managers.

The Marketing Challenge. To support a professional markup and supply the company with top quality leads, successful remodeling companies rank marketing first and foremost. Most of their marketing programs emphasize the quiet, but effective techniques of projecting a high quality image, keeping a high profile, staying active in their community, and generating happy clients and satisfied employees to attract the all-important referral leads. In Chapters 7,8 and 9, we target what you need to do and how you need to do it to generate high quality referral-type leads.

The Employee Challenge. Small businesses used to have difficulty attracting top-quality employees. Superstars worked for big corporations where their security was assured. No more. The employment picture has never been brighter for small businesses who want to hire superb office and managerial staff.

The story is different for the field. Today's demographics show fewer young workers in the marketplace. Booming economic times in many parts of the country have brought the unemployment rate to historic lows. Yet the remodeler needs high-quality employees, those that are well-trained and service-oriented. To attract and keep such workers you must create an effective working atmosphere, supply monetary and non-monetary incentives, and—above all—provide training. In Chapter 4 we focus on hiring and creating superstar team members.

The Quality Challenge. Invariably, successful full-line remodelers across the country sell and deliver high-quality work. But how can growing companies meet this challenge? How can remodeling production be systematized to assure that high quality is the norm? How can workers be trained to do tasks right the first time? This challenge is a critical but difficult one, especially for beginning remodelers. Delivery of quality must permeate every area of your business and so this book focuses, chapter after chapter, on bringing quality and consistency to everything you do. There is a special focus on production in Chapters 12 to 14.

The Customer Satisfaction Challenge. Full-line remodelers cannot be successful without significant numbers of referral leads from delighted clients. No job can be profitable if the customer is unsatisfied and angry. Yet remodeling is one of the most difficult businesses in which to achieve and keep customer satisfaction. In Chapter 14 we target reliable delivery of what the client wants when the client wants it.

Meeting These Seven Challenges

Many remodelers come from a carpentry background. If that is your history, be careful not to buy into the "all I need to do is build well, and people will be happy to pay me the money I deserve and need" philosophy. Right now, if that conviction is in your mind, stamp it out. It's wrong and the roads of remodeling are littered with thousands of failed businesses to prove it.

Getting people to pay you the money you both need and deserve is very tricky and is the basic riddle that every business owner must solve. Meeting these seven challenges will lead you to develop a true business: one in which the client is coaxed and tempted and made to feel good about giving you the right amount of money for the changes they want in their home or office.

No business is ever perfect. The remodeler is often so preoccupied with basic survival that meeting these challenges can be frustrating and difficult. But it must be done! So let's get going.

2

▪ ▪

You: The Remodeler

A small remodeling company's most precious resource is its owner. Your company's success or failure will rest on how you balance and juggle all the hats you are supposed to wear. In any one day, you may act as leader, manager, investor, worker and just plain human being who needs a personal life.

To maximize your worth in the company, focus on these six issues:

O What is my role as worker?

O What is my role as leader?

O How can I bring topnotch new ideas into the company?

O How can I manage my time since I will be fighting overwork?

O How can I manage the stress of being a busy entrepreneur?

O How can I balance my personal and business needs?

Your Role as Worker

Until a remodeling company has a multi-million dollar volume, the owner usually carries two heavy duties. They are responsible for a job—that is, they have front line responsibilities as a worker in the company—and they must be a manager/ leader. Here's how your day-to-day responsibilities can be expected to break out as the company grows:

Up to approximately $150,000 to $200,000 in volume: the owner usually works as a carpenter, does all the selling, administering and production management. It's not uncommon for the owner to feel most "productive" working at the jobsite. They often believe that the money made as a carpenter is the most beneficial for their company. Because of all the varied duties, the owner may work 60-70 hours a week. Sometime during the next growth spurt, the owner will hire office help to relieve some of the paperwork burdens.

From $200,000 to approximately $500,000-600,000 in volume: the owner is no longer working in the field, but still handles all selling, administering and production management. They have brought in an office manager/assistant. At somewhere near $500,000 in volume, the owner often hires a management level person to take over sales or production management because the owner is feeling very overworked.

From $500,000 to approximately $1,000,000 in volume: the owner handles two of the three main management functions (sales, administration, or production management). At $1 million, the owner often hires a second management level person to take over—totally or partially—one of the two remaining functions they are handling.

These volume ranges are just guidelines. It is interesting to note that the larger the average job size, the higher the volumes that can be attained before the owner hands off part of his/her work. The smaller the average job size, the lower the volume before the handoff is made.

☞COACHING TIP

Remodeling owners who retain the sales function rather than the production manager job, tend to be more successful than those whose main talents are in production alone. This is true for two reasons. Clients like to buy from an owner whom they believe will deliver on their promises. Secondly, top sales talent is very difficult to find in remodeling. However, if you don't like selling and don't feel you are good at it, you'll have to hand it off.

Most remodelers have a full time job on the front line. While you might be able to complete your tasks in 40 hours, it may take an employee much longer. Remember this as you hire employees to handle parts of your work.

Why is this so? It's because you—as company owner—are allowed to handle tasks in a seat-of-the-pants manner because you have all of the pertinent information in your head. However, you want the employee to document and keep a paper trail and handle work within a system. Also, you know exactly how you want things handled. The employee is often trying to figure out how you want them handled.

No matter how important your selling or production management, you have to be careful not to slight your role as owner and leader in the company. This role has been called working *on* your company not just *in* your company.

VOICES OF EXPERIENCE...

Michael Gerber has written a powerful, easy-to-read book that will totally change how you view your relationship to your company. Gerber builds a convincing case that entrepreneurs actually trip themselves up by having a skill like carpentry.

"In fact, rather than being their greatest single asset, knowing the technical work of their businesses becomes their greatest single liability. For if the technician didn't know how to do the technical work of the business, he would have to learn how to get it done. He would be forced to learn how to make the business work, rather than to do the work himself."

Michael Gerber, THE E MYTH REVISITED, HarperBusiness, 1995.

Your Role as Leader

Even more important than the day-to-day job you do in your company, is your role as a leader. The dictionary defines a leader as one who is in charge, one who influences. But what if there are no employees to lead? Your leadership role still exists. You need to see and plan the big picture for your company. Your role is:

1. To provide vision
2. To decide major directions and goals
3. To manage growth
4. To provide example and coaching

To provide vision. The best companies have the owner's style and sense of mission. The business started and succeeded initially because of the owner's methods and approach. The owner's prime role is to see that the business reflects his/her philosophies even as the number of employees climb.

ONE REMODELER'S
MISSION STATEMENT

⫷ Each client will feel that his project is the most important thing we have to do today.

⫷ We will serve current clients better than they expect.

⫷ We will keep in touch with past clients.

⫷ We will ask for referrals.

⫷ We will take work from architects, but we will not compete on price.

⫷ We will develop leads by enhancing our name recognition.

⫷ We will continuously monitor the ways we do things to see if we can find better ways.

⫷ We will learn something every day.

⫷ We will respect our clients.

⫷ We will respect our subcontractors.

⫷ We will respect each other.

⫷ Those we cannot respect will not work for us, nor will we work for them.

⫷ We will manage ourselves to a schedule.

⫷ We will deliver superb workmanship.

⫷ We will deliver value for price charged.

Finley Perry, F.H. Perry Builder, Hopkinton, MA

VOICES OF EXPERIENCE...

"If any one idea about leadership has inspired organizations for thousands of years, it's the capacity to hold a shared picture of the future we seek to create. One is hard pressed to think of any organization that has sustained some measure of greatness in the absence of goals, values, and missions that become deeply shared throughout the organization.

"When there is a genuine vision (as opposed to the all-too-familiar 'vision statement'), people excel and learn, not because they are told to, but because they want to. But many leaders have personal visions that never get translated into shared visions that galvanize an organization. All too often, a company's shared vision has revolved around the charisma of a leader, or around a crisis that galvanizes everyone temporarily. But, given a choice, most people opt for pursuing a lofty goal, not only in times of crisis, but at all times."

Peter M. Senge, THE FIFTH DISCIPLINE,
Doubleday/Currency, NY, NY, 1990.

To decide major directions and goals. If the company is to function as a team, the team needs to know what the game is and the rules of the game. The owner serves as the coach, the goal setter, the big-picture person. He/she must answer such questions as—

What is the dollar volume goal for sales? For profit?

What type of job and what type of customer will the company target?

When should the company add a sales manager, a production assistant, or move to a larger office?

When there's an economic downturn, what is our action plan?

To manage growth. Because rapid growth has proven deadly for many remodeling businesses, a remodeler must manage growth carefully. Capacity has to be raised gradually—10-20% annually at most. Employees need to be trained and prepared to meet the demand. Cash flow needs grow as volume grows and the company should be profitable and stable before moving to a signicantly higher volume.

To provide leadership and coaching. An ancient warrior once said about leadership, "An army of deer led by a lion is more feared than an army of lions led by a deer." Employees are not all self-motivated. They thrive on the new style of leadership—coaching. This style fits with the remodeling firm's agenda—to build a team. When the boss is upset, the employees are upset. When the owner is optimistic and enthusiastic, the employees follow suit. As owner you are watched at all times and your behavior assessed for implications.

VOICES OF EXPERIENCE...

"The personality and character of a small business owner has a big impact on a company's environment and on whether employees care about quality, customer satisfaction and the success of the business. Successful leaders...focus on the areas where they're strong and surround themselves with people whose strengths offset their own weaknesses."

Robert H. Rosen, LEADING PEOPLE: TRANSFORMING BUSINESS FROM THE INSIDE OUT, Viking Press, 1996.

Bringing Innovation to Your Company

Find a successful remodeling company and you'll find a company that is focused on innovation—on finding that next good idea that can be adapted to solve a problem. Go to your local bookstore and find the books focused on the issues of change and innovation. You'll find a huge stack. Why are these such important issues? Because the rate of change has accelerated enormously. Change is driven by the dissemination of information. Our access to information is now staggering and is expected to continue to increase exponentially.

Let's review some amazing statistics cited in *New Work Habits for a Radically Changing World* (Pritchett & Associates, Inc., Dallas, TX):

- A weekday edition of The New York Times contains more information than the average person was likely to come across in a lifetime during 17th century England.

- There has been more information produced in the last 30 years than during the previous 5000.

- Let's say you are going to a party, so you pull out some pocket change and buy a little greeting card that plays "Happy Birthday" when it's opened. After the party, someone casually tosses the card into the trash, throwing away more computer power than existed in the entire world before 1950.

- In fact, you are probably wearing more computing power on your wrist than existed in the entire world before 1961.

- The number of cellular phone subscribers had jumped from zero in 1983 to 16,000,000 by the end of 1993.

How are you tapping into this information whirlwind—this explosion? If you've had the opportunity to look into the materials available on the Internet, you're likely to be overwhelmed by how much you can access. Information leads directly to change. The more we open the windows of our minds to information, the more we will change what our companies are doing.

VOICES OF EXPERIENCE...

"I am always searching for the next good idea. I wait until I hear it from a couple of different sources. Usually the idea that catches your attention is a solution to an ongoing problem that your company has. I hold a meeting, talk about the new solution and sell it a bit. Then I delegate the new solution to the appropriate person."

Jerry Roth, G. M. Roth Design Remodeling, Inc., Nashua, NH

Overcoming information isolation. Remodelers often feel isolated. If a problem arises—like no cash in the checkbook, the need for more information on the lead carpenter system, a poor job description for office manager—you may feel you have to invent the solution. The good news is that you don't. Help is everywhere. Here are some resources:

- Join an association. Most major cities have a local chapter of one of the two main associations: the *Remodelors Council* of the *National Association of Home Builders* (NAHB-RC), or the *National Association of the Remodeling Industry* (NARI). Both are headquartered in the Washington, D.C. area. If you don't have a local chapter available, you can join either group as a member-at-large.

- Start an informal breakfast club with other remodelers. You may decide not to share your innermost financial secrets with potential local competitors but you can share lots of resources and information.

- Check into a national peer membership group like *Remodelers Executive Roundtables,* open to the over $750,000 remodeler. The last few pages of this book list more information on this powerful program.

- Subscribe (often it's free) to the trade publications like *Remodeling* magazine (based in Washington, DC), *Qualified Remodeler* (based in New York) and *Journal of Light Construction* (based in Vermont).

- Purchase books and educational materials. Remodeling Consulting Services, Inc. (301-588-8172), The Home Builder Press (Washington, DC), HomeTech (Bethesda, MD) and *The Journal of Light Construction* (Vermont) all carry quality materials. If you get 1 or 2 good ideas from your purchase—and you're likely to get many more—you've got a bargain.

- Keep an eye out for the hot general business books. Usually the top 10 books each year are worth reading. If you buy a book and find it hard going, move on to the next book.

- There are a number of regional and national conventions which feature remodeling. They often combine a trade show with educational seminars, and they can provide an inexpensive yet excellent learning experience. At these meetings you can get away from the details of your business to take a look at the larger picture of how your business could operate better.

◄■ Audiotapes are a perfect medium for remodeler education. Plunk a meaty business tape in your tapedeck as you head off to a client meeting. Arrive motivated and ready-to-go. Business tapes are available in many places ranging from your local bookstores to major national sellers. Convention courses are often recorded and can be purchased on site or ordered later.

◄■ Remodeling sales, marketing, and project management seminars make the rounds of the country. Go ahead and take a day off to gather new information. You'll return to your business refreshed and ready to solve some knotty problems.

Follow German General Bismarck's advice to keep ahead of everyone else in your market. He said "Fools say they learn from experience. I prefer to learn by others' experience."

☞ **COACHING TIP**

Set aside a budget equal to 1-2% of your sales volume to invest in your education and that of your staff.

Innovate with a little help from your friends. In many remodeling companies owners see themselves as the prime innovators. But in really successful companies the owner involves each and every employee in continuous improvement. Keep everyone who works for you focused on finding improvements—no matter how small.

The Japanese are superb in getting employee input. On average, Japanese employees submit 32.4 ideas per year per worker with an implementation rate of 87%. Compare this to

US employees who submit an average of .17 ideas per worker (1 idea every 6 years) with an implementation rate of 32%. This gives Japanese companies a 22-fold advantage in net savings per 100 eligible employees.

VOICES OF EXPERIENCE...

"Organizations can't stop the world from changing. The best they can do is adapt. The smart ones change before they have to. The lucky ones manage to scramble and adjust when push comes to shove. The rest are losers and they become history."

Price Pritchett, NEW WORK HABITS FOR A RADICALLY CHANGING WORLD,
Pritchett & Associates, Dallas, TX, 1994

But what does all this information and input mean to you? Why should you stay well read, well associated and up-to-date? Because:

- your next good idea already exists
- the solution to your most difficult problem has been invented
- your mind needs to be global, to be visionary—it needs constant new input to stay active and creative.

Inventing solutions within your company—from scratch—is inefficient and it may not be that good a solution anyway. Stay on top of your industry, in touch with your peers and do lots of creative swiping/sharing if you want to be successful.

VOICES OF EXPERIENCE...

Jim Strite of Strite Remodeling Co. in Boise, Idaho, is an information/education maven who reads 24 business books a year. What does he do with ideas?

"I put the idea out to my team, get feedback, brainstorming as to the advantages and disadvantages. We look at the resources needed. If we intend to implement the idea, we put it in writing as a goal along with who is going to do it and by when. We follow up at each meeting to see if they are on track. That's how we do it."

So much has been written about the necessity of staying creative and innovative. Here are some other voices:

...the people who succeed in business don't do so because of what they know, but because of their insatiable need to know more. Conversely, the problem with most failing businesses I've encountered is not that the owners don't know enough about finance, about marketing, about management, about operations—they don't, but those things are easy enough to learn. The problem is that they think they know enough. And so they spend their time defending what they know, rather than discovering what they don't."

Michael Gerber, THE E MYTH REVISITED, HarperBusiness, 1995.

If the right people have the right information at the right time, problems will be solved by them."

Riaz Khadem and Robert Lorber, ONE PAGE MANAGEMENT, Quill, NY, NY, 1986.

Our directive to you is to observe, look, listen, and borrow, borrow, borrow from the best."

John L. Stanton, Richard J. George, SUCCESS LEAVES CLUES, SLC Associates, Lindenwold, NJ, 1994.

" A mind that is stretched to a new idea never returns to its original dimensions."

Oliver Wendell Holmes

" The ability to learn faster than your competitors may be the only sustainable competitive advantage."

Arie De Geus, head of planning for Royal Dutch/Shell quoted in THE FIFTH DISCIPLINE, Peter M. Senge, Doubleday/Currency, NY, NY 1990.

Not only is constant learning your competitive edge, it is also what today's workers want to fulfill their lives. You have everything to gain by opening the windows and doors of your business to new ideas.

Maximizing Your Time

It seems that everyone we meet is overworked. But remodelers tend to be outrageously overworked. They have too much to do and too little time to do it. The key diagnostic question is:

Are you mismanaging the time you have or do you have just too much work to fit into your time?

Usually the answer is both. Let's attack them one at a time.

Too Much Work? How many jobs are you doing and how many roles are you playing? We can solve overwork by analyzing your highest value to the company. Keep a two week log of your worktime in 15 minute increments. Every time you finish a task write down the time and a short description of what you were doing. At the end of two weeks add up the various major categories. They might include material takeoffs, site visits, client phone contacts, designing, and sales meetings. Are there any tasks on your list that someone else in your company earning less than $14 an hour could handle? Are there any tasks that someone outside the company could do for the same sum?

ANALYZING JACK'S TIME

For two weeks, remodeler Jack has kept a log of how he spent his time. He averages the information to get an idea of how he is spending his hours in a given week. Here's what he found:

SALES	HOURS PER WEEK
sales meetings	6
estimating	7
taking leads	1
designing	8
misc.	3
SUBTOTAL	25
ADMINISTRATIVE	
produce contracts	3
answer phones	1.5
misc.	4
SUBTOTAL	8.5
PRODUCTION	
client phone calls	3
client meetings	4
contact subs	5
site visits	16
material take offs/orders	6
material pick up	6
SUBTOTAL	40
TOTAL AVERAGE HOURS PER WEEK:	**73.5**

Jack is working at an untenable pace. He may be somewhat less than perfect in how he manages his time—in fact people who are this busy are often juggling what they are doing to meet today's deadlines and are inefficient as well. Here are some ideas for Jack that have worked for other remodelers.

His designing could be farmed out to a part-time draftsperson. Jack would continue to do the conceptual design. His word processing, as in producing contracts, could also be done by others as long as the "boilerplate" contract was composed and ready to be adapted. His field personnel could help with subcontractor calls, takeoffs, material orders and those material pickups that are unavoidable. These three production changes would save Jack up to 17 hours a week.

Consider your time as owner worth at least $50 an hour. Use that figure to decide who will pick up the box of screws, check a window price or proofread a letter. If anyone else can do it, let them.

Just as delegation and subcontracting helps Jack, focus on getting any employees you have to be reliably responsible for their job. When people are hired to manage activities, train them well and then step back. Continue to supervise, set goals, budget and read reports. Otherwise, let the employee handle their work. This lets you handle the work only you can handle.

Some remodelers have been burned by handing off and then having the employee drop the ball. Learn to make periodic reviews of progress or create "windows" on the work of others to check their performance against the goals you have set with them. Such windows will alert you to problems that could arise or assure you that the employee is right on track.

No amount of time management efficiency can relieve the overwork of handling too many tasks. That calls for delegating, hiring, omitting, or subbing. You must get rid of some of the work you are handling.

Need Better Time Management? However, if you do need to manage the time you have more efficiently, there's lots of help and tips. Each of us has our own style of working and needs to pick solutions that match our way of doing things. Here are some solutions you may want to consider:

☞ Consider a four day (10 hour day) work week for the field. That will leave you with one extra day to do office/sales/ estimating/paperwork. Many remodelers have found moving to this system an absolute joy in helping them solve their time problems because it allows you to focus without interruption.

☞ Focus on tasks in larger blocks of time. Many remodelers find that dedicating certain parts of the week to certain tasks allows them to work more efficiently. For instance a remodeler may dedicate two half days a week to selling and estimating and three mornings to visiting job sites. Some remodelers leave their office (and phone), take off their beeper, and go to the library to work quietly during some part of the week. Today's go-everywhere communication systems can mean you are never uninterrupted if you don't "unhook" at some point.

☞ COACHING TIP

True time management results from recognizing the important as distinct from the urgent. The urgent screams for attention. The important is usually very quiet. Mr. Harris is pestering you to get his job done. The budget and business plan and marketing plan can wait another day....and another....and another. How you choose to spend your working hours could be the most important choice you make in your business.

☞ If you start a task, try to complete it within the same time block. Do you find yourself looking at a new prospective job and then trying to do the estimate two weeks later? You have trouble remembering the details of what the house even looked like. Or do you start an estimate one day and finish it a week later? It takes discipline but don't start it if you can't finish it right away.

☞ If you have others in your office in crowded space, isolate your desk so that you can't see or hear them most of the time. One remodeler's office had gotten so crowded that he and his staff wore earphones and listened to music to try to isolate themselves. If your personnel are good enough to work for you, they are good enough to work without minute-by-minute supervision.

- Avoid procrastination. Make decisions after gathering a suitable amount of information on a particular problem or situation. Handle it promptly.

- Do your hardest work when you are at your best. For some people prime time is early morning—for others it's late afternoon. Your prime time should be used for your toughest industrial-strength work. Use your poorest quality working time to catch up on reading, simple correspondence, ordinary phone calls.

- Insist that all meetings have an agenda and a specified start and stop time.

- Avoid cluttering your mind with information that can be stored and better organized elsewhere. Consider using a scheduling book with room for addresses, appointments, and lists of items to-do. Or find a good computer personal scheduling program and use it. Starting this habit can be difficult, but it soon becomes indispensable.

- Each day before you leave your desk, straighten it and create a prioritized list of to-dos for the next day.

- Try to handle work only once. That includes paperwork, a decision or an issue. Avoid reading the letter, considering it, and putting it aside to handle later.

- Establish A-B-C priorities for paperwork by sorting it into three piles on your desk. The A pile is the most urgent, handle it first. The B pile is less urgent and comes second in priority. The C pile probably will be trashed because it gets outdated.

VOICES OF EXPERIENCE...

"The Information Age has really only just begun. The tools by which we access and process information will be even more dazzling in the years ahead. The proliferation of information will continue unabated. Our ability to harness it to full advantage will depend on how well we adjust our work habits and take charge of our individual information destinies."
John P. Guttenburg Jr., WASHINGTON BUSINESS JOURNAL, 5/26/95.

Guttenburg contrasts our high technology office and the explosion of information and suggests we alleviate information anxiety by improving our work habits:

1. Do it now–touch things only once.
2. Know what to look for so you can filter out information that's unneeded.
3. Don't be an infosaver–95% of information is worthless after you read it once.
4. Get off lists for unsolicited mail or calls. Drop subscriptions that don't regularly bring valuable information.
5. Set up a system that works for you.
6. Plan by the week, work by the hour.

Battling Stress

Any business that is so dependent on schedules and on orchestrating a multitude of people and materials to make the job successful is bound to be stressful. Combine that with the fact that many companies work on too low a markup resulting in constant cash flow concerns. Then mix in the level of overwork that many remodelers sustain, and you have the recipe for burnout. Here's a six-step prescription for battling debilitating stress:

1. First and most important, make the company profitable. Money means you are well paid. Money means you can hire the right number of staff. Money means you can solve the client problem without feeling it will sink the company. Money allows you to relax.

2. Second, develop a sensible schedule that keeps both business and personal life in balance.

3. Hire excellent people who can be trusted to do their best. Then delegate to them so you are relieved of much supervision.

4. Keep your mind fit. Pursue other interests. Read, relax, enjoy family and friends. When you feel yourself getting uptight, take the action (go walking, exercise, meditate) to cool down.

5. Keep your body fit. Eat well and regularly. Don't skip lunch. Avoid eating at your desk. Exercise regularly.

6. Understand how business fits into your total life. Get too serious about business and everything else will get out of kilter.

Aesop's fables include a story about the impoverished farmer and his wife who owned some geese. Each day they would collect the eggs from the nests and sell them at the local market. One day, the farmer collected his eggs and to his amazement discovered an egg of pure gold. The next day, the same goose had laid another golden egg. And so it happened day after day.

The farmer and his wife became rich and greedy. They decided they wanted all the golden eggs all at once. Thus the farmer slaughtered his very special goose so he could collect all the eggs. Needless to say, it didn't work and they lost the valuable daily eggs they had come to count on and fell back into poverty.

Owners of remodeling companies are like the goose that laid the golden egg. They are the company's greatest asset and must be treasured and nurtured. If they burnout or become discouraged or disheartened, the company dies.

VOICES OF EXPERIENCE...

A conversation on Remodeling Online included this question "Do you think there is such a thing as a business 'Munchhausen' syndrome?...That is, an owner who may not even realize it but has an underlying emotional need to be the provider/hero/protector/rescuer and therefore unwittingly causes things to occur in the company so that he or she can be the one to 'swoop down and rescue' the firm?" It's a thought.

Owner Rewards

The issue of nurturing the company owner is a critical one. Remodeling is a business that can be abusive to the owner if important steps aren't taken to be sure that the owner gets the proper pay, works the right hours and generally, enjoys work. Unfortunately, others can't nurture and care for you. You have to do it for yourself. Here's what you should be doing!

Compensation. Try both these rules on your company to assess the <u>minimum</u> you should be earning from your company. Compare your two answers and use the highest number as a guideline.

1. 10% of annual volume

2. Your best carpenter's pay plus $5000

For example, if your company volume is $350,000 annually and your best carpenter makes $25 an hour, the first answer is $35,000 and the second is $55,000 (2,000 hours x $25 = $50,000 + $5000 = $55,000). Thus $55,000 is your minimum pay in your market—but only the minimum, can you do better?

Benefits. You should receive at least health insurance, the use of a vehicle, and a retirement program.

Hours. Working 55 hours a week on average is a level that avoids burnout.

Leisure. You deserve and should arrange for 2-4 weeks vacation each year. Many remodelers find that breaking vacation into one week increments is about the longest they can be gone at one time. Often remodelers close their businesses between Christmas and New Year's as well.

Role. Try to spend at least 50% of your working time in a role you enjoy. This keeps you energetic, enthusiastic and avoids burnout.

As owner, you get to choose the tasks you want to do in your business. Choose those you do well. Hire someone else to do the others. The best businesspeople focus on their strengths—and let people who are better than they are at a specific task focus on that task.

This chapter is about maximizing your worth as owner to the company. This requires you to focus on issues like your role as frontline worker, your role as leader, and your role as innovator while fighting some of the major entrepreneurial hurdles of work and stress overload at the same time you are maintaining a healthy personal life. That's a big challenge.

3

■ ■

Shaping Your Business

Most remodeling companies grow like weeds. But most remodeling companies fail. A weed finds itself sprouting somewhere and grows helter-skelter to whatever size and shape its resources of sun, water, and space allow.

Many remodelers find themselves all of a sudden "in business" and let whatever resources they have carry them to any size, any shape, without conscious control.

Instead, take control of your business and shape its size, profitability and structure. Industry analysts agree that this control is critical to assuring success and longevity in your business. Having control means making conscious decisions on five critical questions:

1. What type of legal structure will my business take?

2. How will my business be organized?

3. How much volume do I want to do?

4. Do I want a "practice" or a growth-oriented company?

5. What will my business "look" like? Where will my business workplace be? Will the business have a warehouse? Will it have a showroom?

1. Your Business' Legal Structure

The decision of what legal structure your business should have should be based on your concerns about owner's liability, initial cost, government control, income taxes, and the management process desired. No one right answer exists. Be sure to consult an accountant and lawyer to work out the best answer for you. Here's a quick rundown of of five types of legal structure:

Sole Proprietorship

Partnership

Corporation

Subchapter S Corporation

Limited Liability Corporation

Sole Proprietorship

Most remodeling companies begin as a sole proprietorship. The business is owned by one individual who has complete control over it. Taxes are paid on the income from the business through the owner's individual income tax return. It's simple because the business pays no business tax and doesn't file a tax return. But all business liability flows through to the owner with the result that the owner's personal assets are at risk.

Partnership

A partnership may include any number of individuals acting together with the common purpose of making a profit. The parties should sign a formal, written Partnership Agreement. Interest in the partnership may or may not be equally divided. A partnership can have general partners who have control over the business and no limit to their potential loss, and limited partners who have no control over the business and take a limited profit and/or loss.

Taxes are paid on income from the business according to each partner's appropriate share. The partnership files a tax return, but the individual partners are subject to the taxes, not the partnership itself.

C Corporation

A corporation is licensed by the state and is formed by filing Articles of Incorporation. The corporation then operates according to formal bylaws. Ownership is through shares of stock.

Income is paid to stockholders through salary (if they are employees) and dividends. Generally, losses are incurred by the corporation; they are not passed through to the stockholders. Taxes are paid by the corporation on income the business produces, while the stockholders are only responsible for taxes on the money they actually take out of the corporation. Money left in the corporation gets taxed twice—once as corporate earnings and then as individual earnings when it has been paid out. Management of the business is by a board of directors normally composed of members of the firm. Companies today are also beginning to use outside experts on their boards of directors to obtain impartial guidance.

Subchapter S Corporation

This unique corporate status provides a shield against personal liability, and it also avoids some of the tax complexities and consequences of operating as a corporation. Income and loss passes directly through to the shareholder on his or her personal tax return avoiding the possibility of double taxation that is found in the C Corporation. It is obtainable only by small businesses.

Limited Liability Corporation

The limited liability corporation (LLC) combines some of the characteristics of corporations and partnerships. It allows the business owners freedom from personal liability. It also allows multiple owners to allocate profits differently than ownership interests. For example, one owner could receive 35% of the profits, a second owner 25% and the third 40% even though each owner owns one third of the business. LLC's are governed by state law. Many states—but not all—recognize LLC's so be sure to discuss your business with a legal expert to decide which entity best fits your needs.

It's common for remodeling companies to start as sole proprietorships and—as they grow—elect to become corporations. Sometimes this pattern results from a lack of knowledge rather than a considered decision. Be sure you are familiar with the various structures your business can take and make a thoughtful decision.

2. Patterns of Organization and Growth

There are two critical factors that determine how a company will be organized and how much overhead will be required. They are:

1. Average job size

2. Annual volume

Average Job Size. In theory you can find out what your average job size is by taking your annual volume and dividing it by the number of jobs you've done. That's in theory. But in most companies, you probably need to throw out all those tiny repairs that would skew the average. Or you may have had one outrageously large job last year. Take that one out.

Another way to analyze average job size is to find the answer to the question:

"What's a 'meat and potatoes' job for you?" In other words, what size job are you really set up for? That usually helps cut right through to the correct answer.

As you look at the organizational charts that follow, keep in mind that they best represent remodelers whose average job size runs $20,000-$30,000. If your jobs average higher than that, you'll be able to do more with less, organizationally. In other words, you'll add overhead employees more slowly than the charts show. However, if your jobs average a smaller size, you may need to add those new overhead employees sooner.

Annual Volume. This is an easier question for most remodelers to answer. How much work did they *produce* in the past year?

While organizational charts may seem like a fancy way to express what has already happened in a company, they actually are a wonderfully simple and graphic method of showing what the company looks like—who the employees are, what relationship they have to each other and the owner, and the organizational structure of your company.

Let's explore the four major stages in the growth of remodeling businesses:

- the average company at $150,000 in volume
- the average company at $250,000 in volume
- the average company at $500,000 in volume
- the average remodeling company at $1 million in volume

In particular, keep an eye on how the owner's job description changes.

The $150,000 Company

If your company is $150,000 in volume, you are one busy owner. You work on the job during the day putting in at least 40 hours a week as carpenter. You then have all the selling, designing and estimating to do as well as managing the production. You are unlikely to have any paid help except for a helper on the job at least some of the time.

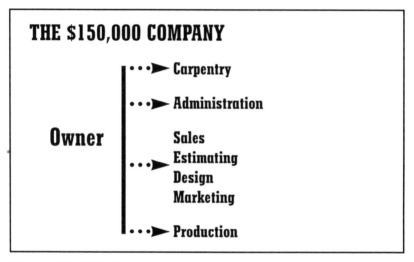

The $250,000 Company

If your produced volume is $250,000, you represent the "average" size remodeling company. If you are well organized (as shown in box) you have left the field work to others and now manage three functions within the firm:

◄ Selling of all jobs

◄ Production supervision of all jobs

◄ General administration (perhaps with a spouse helping part-time).

For the first time in the growth of the company, the owner has an ability to keep new jobs coming down the pipeline and has the time to do some simple marketing to keep new leads coming in. All employees report directly to the owner so there is plenty of troubleshooting to do.

Sometimes, the owner of a company this size has not hired an office person to help—perhaps in a move of false economy. That means that to save perhaps $10.00 an hour, the owner is doing $10.00-an-hour work when $50.00-an-hour work—work only the owner can do—lies waiting.

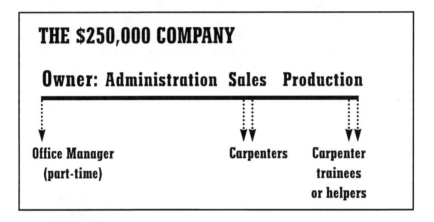

THE $250,000 COMPANY

Owner: Administration Sales Production

Office Manager
(part-time)

Carpenters

Carpenter
trainees
or helpers

The $500,000 Company

At some point around $500,000 in volume, you find yourself becoming very overworked and dropping the ball on important tasks. Now is the time to give up the job of selling or production management. In our example, the owner has hired someone to supervise production and production employees report to this new employee.

Usually remodelers decide to retain the function they enjoy most or the function for which they believe they will have the hardest time hiring a competent replacement for themselves. The best answer for most remodelers is to retain the job of selling. Top salespeople will be your toughest hire throughout the life of your business. Also, retaining production results in more personnel reporting directly to the owner. Production is fraught with time-based crises, meaning you will often have to drop what you are doing to handle an immediate production problem. Retaining the sales function does not have these same drawbacks.

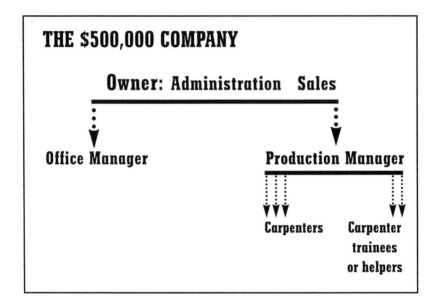

THE $500,000 COMPANY

Owner: Administration   Sales

Office Manager

Production Manager

Carpenters   Carpenter
trainees
or helpers

The $1,000,000 Company

As your remodeling company approaches $1 million in volume, you find yourself spending more and more of your time administering, coaching and troubleshooting throughout the company. That means that production management and sales have to be largely in the hands of others. This also means that most of the employees now report to another direct supervisor—who then reports to you.

Whatever the remodeling company's size, knowing how most remodelers are organized can help a remodeler plan for the future of the company. All employees in a remodeling firm

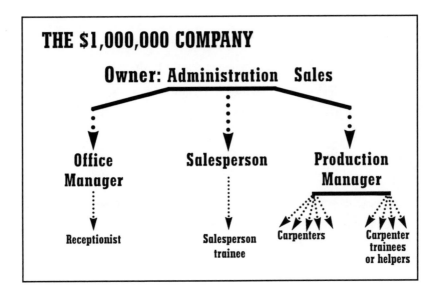

should be able to draw a correct organizational chart in the sense that they know how the basic work is divided among employees and who reports to whom.

As your company grows, continue to control the number of employees who report directly to the owner, so that your position is workable and you do not erode the authority to supervise that you have given others. Insulate yourself from the day-to-day small problems and still keep an "open door" policy. Only in this way will you have time to fulfill your job as leader.

Since these organizational charts largely show employees who are paid in overhead dollars, you can see that as your company grows, so does your overhead. In fact, your overhead usually grows in percentage of volume—not just in the greater dollars associated with greater volume. It's not uncommon for the million dollar company to have an overhead that runs 28%-33% if their average job size falls in that mid-range. Companies never have a lower overhead than when the owner does it all!

COACHING TIP

In our consulting, we often ask the owner to draw a quick organizational chart of their company. Usually what they draw truly represents how they view the organization. If the chart is confused and everybody is shown doing everything, we've found that the organization is inefficient, error-prone and confusing to everyone inside and outside the company. By cleaning up the job descriptions and sorting out all tasks to the person directly responsible, the company often takes a giant leap forward in efficiency and productivity.

3. How Much Volume Do I Want to Do?

Is it strange to think of exactly what volume you want to sell in a year? Many remodelers think it is. They work the leads they get, sell what they sell, and tally up the result. They are victims of their marketplace.

How can you set up a professional company aimed at providing topnotch service to each of your clients when you don't know what your volume will be? We call this the "jellyfish" approach. A jellyfish floats on the surface and eats only when its tentacles comes in contact with food. A jellyfish company floats on the current of their marketplace and makes do with what comes in the door. They don't *make* it happen.

To run a professional company, you have to aim for the right volume target and then take the steps needed to make that volume happen. Sometimes the problem is not that too few people want to buy, but that too many people want to buy. Yes, that is a problem that needs careful analysis and decisions on how to handle the overload. You may decide not to sell to everyone. You may decide to move start dates far out in advance. You may also decide to increase your markup which will give you more money and usually will decrease the workload at least somewhat.

COACHING TIP

Whenever too many prospects want to buy from you, consider it a signal to raise markup at least 5%. Wait another six weeks and if you still are flooded, raise markup another 5%. Continue this strategy until workload fits capacity.

Deciding Average Job Size

Your annual volume is one of the keys to understanding what your company looks like (and should look like) at any given time. The second key is average job size. Let's say you have a company that does $500,000 a year in volume. Your average job size is $100,000+. You do 5 jobs each year. Your company needs a minimum of leads (you probably spend less than 1% on marketing), a small amount of selling and has only 5 sites to visit over the 12 months.

But what if your average job is $2,000—and you also want to produce $500,000 in volume? You need nearly 1,000 leads. Your marketing budget is likely to be 8-10%. Your sales force must sell 250 jobs and they are spread all over town. You're working with 250 buyers and ordering for all those jobs.

Either company can be highly successful. But they have very different organizations. In fact, the company with large jobs can be managed by an owner who does all the selling and production management. The small job company may need two salespeople, a production manager and someone to spend lots of time on marketing and administration.

You can choose. And you can change. Whenever you go from smaller to larger jobs, you simplify your organization but increase the personalization of service. You also move into a market where the price pressure is even greater.

Let's look at what a small change in average job size can mean. Joe Harris is a $500,000 remodeler. His jobs average $15,000 and he needs to sell 33 jobs a year. If he works to change his average job size by marketing larger jobs, selling up, qualifying out the small job buyer, he should be able to move his average job size to $20,000. Then he only needs 25 jobs a year to make his volume. That's a significant reduction of organizational work for him and his company.

Setting volume goals and targeting your average job size can significantly shape your remodeling company. Most entrepreneurs overlook these important tools. You can use them to drive your company to where you want it to be.

4. Do I Want a "Practice" or a Growth-Oriented Company?

Our natural tendency is to think "bigger is better" as we plan our company's future. But that is not necessarily true. What is true is that we should carefully plan our company's size because that can make the difference between profitability and loss.

At the point your company is doing as much work as it can comfortably do, keeping all employees working to capacity, it is likely to be profitable. Add $50,000 more in volume and you may be forced to add employees to the overhead for only a little more business. Being the "wrong" size can cost you money.

There is a level of growth that represents the most profitable size for an owner who doesn't want to grow beyond his/her own ability to sell and manage production. That is called a *practice*. Your dentist is probably a practice. She has others who work for her, like the receptionist, the bookkeeper, the dental hygienist. The dentist is the main frontline money earner—everyone else is part of her team. But if the dentist became incapacitated for a long period of time, the office would close. In the remodeling practice, the owner is the main money producer—everyone else is a team member dependent on the remodeler's abilities.

VOICES OF EXPERIENCE...

After Linda Case wrote a *Remodeling* magazine column on Practices, she received this e-mail from a reader. "It took me ten years to develop the business plan you laid out in one article. What you described is my business exactly. Over the years I let my testosterone develop my business plan and guess what...everyone got paid but me. Now, I pick the best jobs, market myself to well defined market segments, keep one key man, a few part-time crew men and of course one indispensible office manager/assistant/bookkeeper.

"Now when I am walking on the Champs Elysees or laying on the beach in Montego Bay I look around and guess who is there with me...Doctor, Dentist, Doctor, Dentist."

Why would you want to develop a practice? Because it's a low risk way to make the maximum return with the simplest business to administer. For most remodelers, running a practice is their road to success. Follow three key rules to develop your practice and receive maximum gain:

1. Take your annual volume to the comfortable maximum but don't wear yourself out or burn out any employees. It's not unusual for a practice with a moderate average job size to achieve a $750,000 to $1 million volume.

2. Most importantly, charge a professional level markup between the range of 50-70%. This allows you to be paid for your job as salesperson, production manager and administrator. A 50% markup should achieve a 33% gross profit to be used for paying overhead (including the owner's salary) and net profit. $750,000 in volume at a 50% markup would produce $250,000 in gross profit. The owner might well pay himself/herself $150,000 of the $250,000 under that scenario.

3. Grow no larger than the volume that allows you to comfortably handle all the sales and production management. However, feel free to develop a team to help increase that volume. That team might include an office manager/bookkeeper and a purchaser/designer. The owner might bring in an outside person to help handle the marketing on a subcontracted basis.

Practice Problems

As with all good things, there are tradeoffs. What are the drawbacks of a practice?

- A practice is dependent on the owner at all times. The owner can go on vacation, and should go on vacation, but sales will stop for that period. If the owner became disabled and unable to work for a substantial period of time, the business could fail.

- The practice is not saleable because the business is gone when the owner leaves.

- Although you can develop a nice income as the owner of a practice, there is a limit to how much can be earned from a $500,000-$1,000,000 company. There is greater earning potential—and greater risk—from a larger, multi-million dollar company.

There are drawbacks to running a practice but for many remodelers the pros outweigh the cons. For 90% of today's remodelers, developing a practice represents the very best opportunity for low risk and high gain.

5. Where Will My Company Workplace Be?

It's very likely that you started with a home-based office—most remodelers do. Some homes have enough space to provide a productive working environment; others may not. A well-designed home office can be as up-to-date and efficient as leased space. It can be outfitted with a computer, copier, multiple phone lines, and even a fax machine, and it can make a professional statement particularly for those remodelers who work largely by referral. There's nothing wrong with working in a home office.

Be sure to check with your accountant as to whether you are able to pay rent to yourself and whether you are eligible for a home office tax deduction as these rules seem to change constantly.

If a home-based office becomes less satisfactory as the company grows, you may want to rent or buy commercial office space. This decision can have many rewards:

- A separate office provides a more professional atmosphere for prospective customers and employees. An office outside the home instills confidence in prospective customers and shows that the company is established and not a fly-by-night operation.

- Having a separate business office can provide an economic and marketing advantage. It is usually in a commercial area where the company has better exposure, and where you can attract walk-in or drive-by trade from people who see the sign out front.

VOICES OF EXPERIENCE...

A West Coast remodeler and his staff resorted to wearing radio earphones in order to concentrate as the company grew and added employees. Finally, the remodeler made the decision to move to downtown office space. "We are in our new offices," he wrote just after moving, "which is great and feels like the right thing to have done. The office is in a very visible spot, which has already brought us some attention."

- Better working conditions can save time and money. Without a commercial office that the consumer can visit, you go to the customers' homes for all discussions of proposed jobs. With a separate office you can now invite the customers to come to you for the second visit to discuss the proposal. Now your clients are away from the possible distractions of children, television, pets, and unexpected callers. You appear more professional, have more control of the situation, and can more easily keep the customers' focus on your proposal.

- Promoting the office location prompts some prospects to simply drop by to discuss a job, especially people who are uneasy about inviting a stranger into the house. Once they have met and talked with you or another salesperson, they are less leery of arranging an appointment in their home.

- Most importantly, many remodelers who have moved from a home office to commercial space also find that the business makes fewer demands on their personal lives.

As a business diversification, some remodelers build their own small office buildings or remodel an existing one. In either case, the exterior and the interior of the office will look more professional than an office in a home can be. Building or remodeling an office also provides an opportunity to show what your company can do. Consider making office space a mini-showroom by using different cabinets, countertops, types of lighting that you can show your clients to help them with their own selections. Remodelers often find this office/showroom combination an excellent investment.

Do I Need a Warehouse?

Many smart remodelers refuse to have warehouse space. They believe it is an unnecessary expense and actually will encourage the storage of items that cannot be easily monitored, may get damaged, and ultimately will cost the company money. Instead they buy on an as-needed basis and return any unneeded material, even if they must pay a restocking charge.

Other remodelers believe they need storage space to store materials purchased in quantity, store mis-purchases, and reusable items removed from jobs. The remodeler should be aware of the actual cost of this luxury and decide whether the business can afford it.

The bottom line is that most remodelers have at least some limited warehouse space. Think carefully about your storage needs.

Do I Want a Cabinet Shop?

Many remodelers have cabinet shops to provide the special millwork, cabinets, and built-in items that are so frequently needed in remodeling. However, not all of these remodelers insist—as they should—that the cabinet shop expenses and income be carefully monitored to be certain it is a profit-making center for the company. Any remodeler considering a cabinet shop should treat this as an independent business and set an expense budget, project the volume of work needed to provide a profit for the company and monitor how that profit is achieved. If it's not profitable, the company would be better off buying the millwork and cabinetry from a subcontractor.

☞ COACHING TIP

Most remodelers lose money on their cabinet shops. Don't consider having a shop unless you can make money on it and unless it adds vital prestige to what you do. If you are convinced you should have such a shop, investigate whether there is a market for you to sell your cabinetry to others as well as to your own company's clients. When selling to your customers, be sure you earn the subcontractor's profit on your cabinets. In other words, sell to yourself at a marked up price—even if you do give your company a better discount than an outside buyer.

While all this might make a cabinet shop sound impossible, there are remodelers that make a real success of their ability to construct their own cabinetry. A Rocky Mountain remodeler has a cabinet shop that builds products for their own company, other contractors and consumers. In fact, the shop's ability to do very unusual custom work often leads to a custom home job or other unique remodeling projects. So the shop is not only a money maker—but also a marketing tool.

Do I Need a Showroom or Selection Room?

Every now and then you read that soon "all remodelers will need showrooms."

Not true. Suppliers are furnishing better showrooms than ever and you can develop a relationship with a supplier's representative who will take excellent care of your client and help them select what is specified.

You should not even consider opening a showroom unless your annual volume is $1 million or more. And you should not consider opening a showroom unless you have interviewed a number of remodelers who have showrooms and can give you insight into what it will entail.

VOICES OF EXPERIENCE...

An East Coast remodeler with a showroom notes how much it can change your operation. "Having a showroom open to the public is totally different from the remodeling business. You now are in the retail business—with walk-in traffic, on-site product sales and a business that must be tended constantly through long retail hours, including Saturdays and weekends."

Whether or not you open a showroom, you'll still want to encourage your clients to make as many selections as possible at your office. Have samples of your standard products and showcase common details in your office. Thus you might want your office to include different types of lighting, countertop surfaces, cabinetry, and flooring to show the client. Most clients don't want to travel to numerous locations to pick out every item on their job. They do want to devote time and attention to a few items and then expedite the choices on selections that are not as important to them.

Making Your Choices

You are in control of your business—many times to a greater degree than you think. Choose wisely and chart your course carefully. By doing so you will have met the Growth Challenge.

4

■ ■

Developing Your Superstar Team

Remodeling is a team activity. At the end of the project, no one person can say they were totally responsible. For your company to be successful, all your employees must be working together toward the same goal.

A team is only as good as its weakest player. A remodeler is only as good as his/her weakest employee. Thus, the hiring, motivating, and training of personnel becomes critical in a small business. Every employee is a key employee. Even your lowest paid worker will have considerable impact on your business and its profitability.

Many entrepreneurs, especially if they have come up from the trades, have limited experience in managing and motivating others. Sometimes a remodeler says "I wish I had a business degree that would have educated me as to how to be a better hirer and trainer and motivator." But the truth is that no degree prepares an entrepreneur for these tasks. You must learn on the job and through the information that you can glean from books, magazines, seminars and the advice of peers.

VOICES OF EXPERIENCE...

"An effective organization is a living thing: An organization is its people. People breathe life and purpose and energy into an organization. An organization has a manner, spirit, tempo, nature, character. It has moods, joys, fears, and sorrows. But most important of all, an effective organization has a purpose that is shared by all its members and to which they willingly commit their efforts. People working together can do almost anything."

James L. Hayes, MEMOS FOR MANAGEMENT: LEADERSHIP, American Management Association, NY 1983

Hiring Well Is a Tough Job

In most parts of the country, the labor market is tighter than ever. This situation results from two economic realities. The current economy is utilizing almost every employable worker. Secondly, the baby boom has passed through, and employers are now seeing the baby bust—a reduced workforce resulting from a time of fewer births. This baby bust means millions fewer workers in the crucial range for field workers—18 to 25 year olds.

VOICES OF EXPERIENCE...

Steve McGee, a consultant in Tustin, CA, cites a survey of 10,000 high school students asked to choose from 252 careers. Construction placed 251st, barely beating out "cowboy." In another study, the NAHB Research Center has found that the average age of skilled labor leaving the industry is at an all-time low of 33.

BUILDER magazine, July, 1996.

Neither of these factors promises to disappear. The only solution is to hire very wisely and be prepared to train more heavily. When you find a superstar, be prepared to market the benefits of working for your company. Good people can always find a job. Why should they work for you? Be sure to consider not just pay and normal benefits but the psychic benefits that your company offers—the atmosphere and culture that makes working for you a pleasure.

As you build your team, consider that your company is very similar to an orchestra. You are the orchestra leader and you may be very good. But if your individual musicians are poor or unmotivated or unwilling to be team players, you can't overcome their ineptitude.

☞ COACHING TIP

The Seinfeld television show is a great example of the benefits of building a strong team. Jerry Seinfeld is certainly the star but he is strongly supported by Kramer, George, Elaine and Newman who are strong stars in their own right. And they are all further supported by the excellent character actors who play parents and dates and doctors and friends. When you are hiring, think of yourself as casting a very important part in your company. Don't settle for the best of the worst. Go for a superstar.

Superstars are employees who are outstanding at their job. In order to have and keep superstars you must first find and hire them. Here are six steps for hiring successfully.

1. Write an accurate job description

2. Develop an employee handbook

3. Recruit creatively

4. Qualify carefully

5. Prepare for the interview

6. Interview for both aptitude and attitude

A continuing theme in this book is the emphasis on early planning to avoid more serious problems later. Preparation is the key to effective hiring. Notice that five of the above six steps involve getting ready to hire.

☞ COACHING TIP

Be especially careful about your preparation when you are hiring your first salesperson, production manager, or office manager. The new employee does not have an existing job to slip into.

Usually you are turning over one segment of your job to the new employee which makes the transition doubly difficult. While you did a lot of the job instinctively, you now expect the new employee to be orderly and organized. Often the details remain in your head and are difficult to transfer. The failure rate for new employees taking over part of what the boss used to do is very high. Be sure to do the right preparation.

Hiring Step 1: Write an Accurate Job Description

If you want a new employee to succeed, that employee must have an accurate and understandable job description. Start by writing down the procedures you use now and those you want to add. Then consult with other remodelers on how to improve these procedures. Review some current job descriptions—in the library, if need be—before writing a final job description. Remember that job descriptions change. They are living documents that should be reviewed regularly.

Having accurate job descriptions has four major effects:

◀ They force you to analyze the type and quantity of work to be done and the procedures and methods to be utilized. In creating a job description, don't just put on paper what you've been doing. The writing of a job description should prompt you to examine and evaluate the responsibilities, duties, and procedures that you want your employee to assume and commit to.

◀ The job description clearly informs a new employee or existing employee of what is expected of them. A job applicant can review the job description and either commit to it or agree that the job may not be suitable for him/her. Workers agree that they want an accurate, understandable job description for their position.

◀ Over the years, a job description can save a remodeler considerable time explaining and re-explaining the job responsibilities and duties.

◀ A job description increases the likelihood of hiring success because both employer and employee understand and have agreed on the job responsibilities and duties.

Hiring Step 2: Develop an Employee Handbook

Every company with employees should have an employee handbook. A few hours spent to develop a simple manual will reward you many times over with fewer misunderstandings and less on-the-job training. Without a manual most employees learn by hearing, "Oh, we don't do things that way in our company," after they've already made a mistake. With a little advance preparation, the missteps and the embarrassment could be avoided.

Here are some of the topics you'll want to cover in your employee handbook:

- Company mission and philosophy
- Organizational chart and chain of command
- Equal Employment Opportunity statement
- Employment and separation policies
- Recruitment and hiring
- Immigration Reform Act
- Periodic performance evaluations
- Standards of conduct and disciplinary actions
- Sexual harassment policy
- Personal appearance standards
- Personal use of company tools, vehicles, and equipment
- Infractions including drugs, alcohol, unexcused absenteeism
- Grievance procedures
- Compensation and benefits
- Working hours, breaks, lunch times
- Pay periods, timecards
- Overtime and compensatory time
- Social Security
- Travel or vehicle allowances
- Insurance benefits
- Workers' Compensation Insurance
- Incentive, profit-sharing, and/or pension program
- Attendance at professional meetings
- Attendance and tardiness

O Various types of leave (including vacations, holidays, sick leave, jury duty, maternity, paternity)

O Safety and security procedures

O Accident prevention

O Reporting on-the-job accidents and injuries

O Fire emergencies

O Smoking policy

O Any tools and equipment the employee must supply

Since a poorly worded employee handbook can be used against you and your company, have your manual reviewed by your attorney. It also should be considered a living document and changed as your policies change. Many companies give each employee a copy and have the employee sign a receipt to show that he/she has read the policy manual.

Hiring Step 3: Recruit Creatively

Do you automatically turn to the classified ads when you have a new job opening? Unfortunately everyone else in town is doing the same. Most applicants reached through the classified ads are currently unemployed or already have an agreement to leave their firms at a specified time. Thus the classified ad pool of workers is somewhat suspect.

Top workers can choose the company they want to work for because they are in demand. Attracting these key people takes creative recruiting and an excellent reputation among industry workers. On the other hand, remodelers with progressive employee policies sometimes have a waiting list of applicants for the next available opening even in areas with labor shortages. That should be your aim in your company.

Consider how you can hire from the ranks of the employed. You could leave flyers on trucks parked at the lumberyard or builder's supply firm and post notices on their bulletin boards. You could advertise an evening open house at which you take applications, have the present employees talk with potential employees, and serve light refreshments. You could set up interviews at the local high school vocational school or carpentry training program.

When you do use a classified ad, it should describe the job accurately and list the attractive benefits or working conditions you offer. Using more space than the other classified ads will make your ad stand out. Consider an ad in your local association newsletter or even in a national trade publication. Put the word out that you have a position open on one of the websites that attract remodelers and their employees.

The key is to be creative in your recruitment of applicants. You might use a company meeting to brainstorm unique ways to attract excellent applicants.

Hiring Step 4: Qualify Carefully

Your recruiting efforts have resulted in letters or resumes (best) or phone calls into your office. Set up a way to assess and qualify the very best candidates for the position. Interview only the best candidates carefully and well. If there are no great candidates, go back to recruiting.

VOICES OF EXPERIENCE...

"Experience shows that of every three employees hired, one makes a solid contribution, one is marginal, and one should not have been hired in the first place."
Richard Pinsker in Hiring Winners, *Small Business Forum, Fall 1994.*

Hiring Step 5: Prepare for the Interview

Interviews stuffed into a busy schedule with no preparation are doomed from the beginning. Spend perhaps 15 to 20 minutes thinking about the job description and writing down a few open-ended questions to which the applicant will have to give a narrative reply. Get the applicant to fill out a job application while waiting for the interview. Plan to give serious applicants a copy of the job description to review and discuss.

Hiring Step 6: Interviewing for Aptitude and Attitude

Focus your interview on obtaining information on the applicant's knowledge as it pertains to the job and on the applicant's attitudes toward work. Technical training is relatively easy, but a poor attitude is difficult, if not impossible, to change. Ask questions, keep the candidate talking and give wide latitude for answers. Richard Pinsker, author of *Hiring Winners* provides some interview questions:

? What sort of people do you enjoy working with?

? Among the people who work for you, whom do you admire the most, and why?

? What bores you about your present job?

? Name all the positive factors about your present company.

? Tell me why you left each of your jobs.

? Give some specific examples of how you solved a difficult problem at work.

? Describe where your career is heading and the direction your life has taken.

? Are you pleased with where you are in life right now?

? What things about yourself are you proud of?

INTERVIEW NO-NO'S

🚫 The applicant's age and the applicant's birthdate (even though a birth certificate or baptismal certificate can be used as evidence of citizenship). Once a person is hired, the birthdate may be legally required for insurance policy purposes.

🚫 The applicant's religion.

🚫 The applicant's birthplace, nationality, native country or language, or those of relatives or close associates.

🚫 How or where the applicant learned the languages he/she speaks, writes, or understands.

🚫 The applicant's sex or marital status.

🚫 Whether the applicant has children or other dependents.

🚫 The applicant's sexual preference.

🚫 Whether the applicant is handicapped or has had a specific disease. Interviewers may ask whether a candidate for a job has any impairments or diseases that would interfere with his/her ability to do any part of the job for which he/she is applying.

🚫 The applicant's photo (However, once a person is hired, photo identification is required for compliance with the Immigration Control and Reform Act of 1986.)

🚫 Tests not legally related to the job requirement. Any test given must be clearly related to job requirements and must be professionally validated as predicting successful performance for the job in question. A typing test is such an allowable test.

A simple agenda for the interview begins by establishing rapport with the candidate with some small talk. Then explain the interview agenda and start questioning. The applicant should talk 80% of the interview time. Review the job description for the position with the applicant and get feedback from the candidate as to how their abilities fit your needs. Discuss compensation if that is appropriate and close the interview. Make very clear notes so that if you are interviewing a number of candidates, you'll be able to refresh your memory on each. Experts on hiring recommend that you create a standard "report card" on which to grade each applicant.

Checking References

It's been said that the closest to perfection a person ever comes is when they are filling out a job application! That's why checking references is so important. It can be tempting to forego checking references since you might assume that the applicant wouldn't have given you the name if the recommendation could be less than excellent. Also, previous employers are afraid they may be sued if they make negative statements about applicants. So check references but listen between the lines and ask careful questions to elicit problem areas. Ask specific questions such as:

? Please describe some strengths and weaknesses. Request both so as to avoid looking as if you are prejudiced against the candidate. However, if the reference gives only strengths and positive qualities, ask again for the weaknesses.

? How often did he/she miss work?

? How did he/she get along with coworkers and with subordinates? Could you give me some examples?

? Did he/she work well without close supervision?

? Was the applicant willing to share his/her knowledge with other employees, answer their questions, and provide guidance?

? Would you rehire this individual?

HIRING SUPERSTAR EMPLOYEES

★ Write a clear job description.

★ Promote from within wherever feasible.

★ Be creative in advertising the position.

★ Develop or buy a good job application form.

★ Have all personnel forms checked by the company attorney beforehand.

★ Request letters or resumes from the applicants.

★ Prepare a list of questions for the interview.

★ Practice interviewing with someone. Ask for feedback.

★ Avoid illegal questions.

★ Ask questions which cannot be answered "yes" or "no."

★ Ask about driving record for liability purposes.

★ Study the appearance of the applicant.

★ Look for good work attitudes such as eagerness, high energy level, willingness to learn, courtesy, as well as knowledge.

★ Can this applicant sell him/herself?

★ Be prepared to sell the top applicant on the company.

★ Ask the applicant what he/she would like to know about the remodeling company and the work. Does the applicant ask intelligent questions?

★ Check references thoroughly.

★ After hiring, prepare to train heavily for the first 1 to 3 months.

Personality Profiles

A number of remodelers use simple personality profiles or other instruments to help them select the best candidate from the final two or three. Usually the employer chooses the qualities that the job requires and then the profile is used to match the best candidate to the job skills. The candidate fills out the profile which is then put through computer analysis by an industrial psychologist or other expert in human resource development. These instruments are no substitute for good hiring procedures but they can help bring a measure of objectivity to the process.

Increasing the Value of Your (People) Assets

As you think about how you hire and who you hire, it's an excellent time to think about growing and improving your staff. Your responsibility as owner, leader and manager includes training, coaching, motivating and rewarding your employees.

The First Month is Crucial

When a new employee is hired, leaving him/her to sink or swim can be a strong temptation. You wouldn't have hired this person unless you were overworked in some area of your business. It's easy to deluge the new arrival with all the paperwork, phone calls, and open items to be handled. Watch out! This approach will assure that they sink.

Instead, designate the first month of the employee's tenure for intensive training and supervision.

COACHING TIP

Don't make this an excuse to justify your lack of training, but we have found that the better the new hire, the more they teach themselves their job. Great employees are aggressive and pull what they need from others. However, this superstar new hire would progress even faster if they had systematic training. The failure of a new employee often is a sign—not just that you let them down—but also that they didn't have the qualities needed to make it in their job.

Resolve to make a decision after the first month (if not earlier) as to whether this new hire is definitely a good choice or should be replaced. Entrepreneurs tend to hang on too long to marginal employees only to fire them in the end. After the first month's intensive training, devote the next two months to less intense training and supervision—but training should not cease.

In fact, training for all employees—and the owner—should continue forever.

If you realize the new employee is an obvious mishire, let him/her go quickly while keeping to the letter of the law on hiring and firing. An employee that is retained should have a full formal evaluation after the first month, to discuss his/her strengths and weaknesses and to set up future performance goals.

☞ COACHING TIP

Consider establishing a "buddy" program in which one of your workers is assigned to help the new hire succeed, to introduce him/her to coworkers, to see that he/she has someone to eat lunch with, and to help them understand the company philosophy, policies, operating style, and procedures. There's more to succeeding in your company than what is written in the policy manual. New employees slowly learn the real "rules of the road" through the grapevine if you don't facilitate it with the buddy system.

Motivating Employees

Motivating employees does not have to be difficult, but it does take some thinking and planning. Here are eight simple and inexpensive ways to thank, praise, and reward your employees:

- Praise is the number one motivator. Make it quick and timely and real.

- Consider designating an Employee of the Month or Salesperson of the Month parking place—the one closest to your office.

- Feature a different employee each month in a display on your office bulletin board.

- Get everyone in the company better acquainted by featuring personal news as well as company news in a lively internal company newsletter. If the newsletter is put in the paycheck envelope, it is more likely to be taken home to the worker's family as well.

- Two tickets to a ballgame or a dinner for two at a special restaurant provides a bonus for your employee, and it allows the employee to share his/her good fortune with a family member or friend.

- Award an extra paid holiday to an employee who has earned a bonus. Give the employee a 3-day paid vacation for two at a resort.

- Bring the entire company together as a family with a summer picnic or holiday party.

- Award incentive bonuses at company meetings so the recipient can enjoy the admiration of his/her peers.

- When you see an employee doing something that calls for a reward, hand them your business card with "Lunch" written on the back. That entitles them to go out to a special lunch with you at a time of their choice.

VOICES OF EXPERIENCE...

Bob Nelson, author of *1001 Ways to Reward Employees* notes that employee rewards and recognition are more important than ever before. Nelson says that "studies show that employees find personal recognition more motivational than money. Yet, it is a rare manager who systematically makes the effort simply to thank employees for a job well done, let alone to do something more innovative to recognize accomplishments."

Bob Nelson, 1001 Ways to Reward Employees,
Workman Publishing Co., Inc., New York, 1994.

Using Incentives, Bonuses, and Profit Sharing

Encourage your employees to work with you to set clear, measurable goals. Use these to monitor performance. You'll find that the more goals the employee meets, the more motivated they will become.

Look for ways that allow you to pay an above-market rate to employees. In order to remain competitive while doing so, tie the additional pay to increased productivity or efficiency.

Historically, the remodeler's sales force has been paid through a commission program usually based on the gross profit of the sold job. The salesperson receives a salary or draw against this commission to smooth out the payments. Traditionally all other employees have received hourly wages or salaries with no bonuses based on goals. Many companies do give a Christmas/holiday bonus to field personnel, but it normally is based on seniority rather than performance.

An increasing number of remodelers are developing some incentive pay particularly for field workers based on meeting or beating the schedule and for job cost goals. Additional methods need to be developed for sharing profits with office employees.

Any incentive program you develop should have four characteristics:

1. It should reward the behavior you want.

2. It ought to be given quickly, soon after it has been earned.

3. It must be easy for employees to understand and monitor.

4. Seventy-five to eighty-five percent of employees in a given category should be able to achieve the goal. The company's objectives will not be achieved if an incentive rewards only the top 10 percent. Everyone else will become discouraged and stop trying.

Your incentive program should motivate employees to become vitally interested in lowering costs, speeding production, and keeping customers happy. In order to fulfill the first two incentive requirements, many companies combine different programs to reach different employees. Thus, a salesperson's commission may be based on the gross profit on each job he/she handles. The production personnel may benefit from any savings they achieve based on the labor estimate, and office personnel bonuses may be determined by the quarterly or semiannual profits earned by the company.

Put Pay in Perspective

No doubt the paycheck is the easiest scorecard for each employee to keep. However, survey after survey shows that while pay is critically important to all employees, even more important are such concerns as whether the firm—

◄ Treats its employees with respect

◄ Supplies them with challenging and interesting work

➤ Gives recognition for top quality work and useful suggestions

➤ Allows employees to think for themselves

VOICES OF EXPERIENCE...

In *Budgeting for a Small Business,* Terry Dickey urges entrepreneurs to decide what they are paying for. These are the choices he offers:

Risk and reward versus security. Do you emphasize security with a salary or hourly wage, or do you prefer commissions and incentives which are riskier for the employee?

Individual achievement versus teamwork. Are incentives for the group or the individual?

Turnover versus longevity. Which does your company reward?

Career development versus position development. Do you encourage rapid promotion or do you expect a long-term commitment to the job?

Stars versus Others. Do you pay significantly above market rate with the goal of hiring the exceptional or do you focus on ways to make average employees effective?

Terry Dickey, BUDGETING FOR A SMALL BUSINESS, Crisp Publications, 1994.

Half International, a large supplier of temporary employees, reports that when 150 managers were asked to name the most common reason employees leave a company, 34% said limited recognition and praise. Compensation ran second at 29%.

If you pay fair market wages or slightly higher, provide the psychic benefits listed above, and develop a profit-based, incentive system to add to the basic wages, you should be able to hire—and keep—the very best employees in your area.

VOICES OF EXPERIENCE...

"There are two things people want more than sex and money...
recognition and praise."

Mary Kay Ash, founder of the Mary Kay cosmetics company

Training Employees

Since perfect employees are in short supply, successful remodelers motivate and train employees to be top performers. This difficult challenge can be met by even a small business with limited resources. Nothing can substitute for personal one-on-one teaching. However, many resources will augment and extend that teaching. Here are eleven training ideas used by successful remodelers:

- Encourage employees to receive and read industry publications. Many are free and require only that you submit a business card or request on your letterhead.

- Purchase the best business and industry books for a company library and encourage employees to read and consult them.

- Purchase outstanding business, sales, and industry audio tapes (as well as a tape player with a plug-in attachment if necessary) so employees can listen as they drive.

- Hold company meetings on a monthly or bimonthly basis. Make them upbeat and educational as well as motivational.

  - Give awards, review some procedures, discuss problem solving, encourage suggestions.

  - Bring in a speakcr from a supplier to present installation or sales tips.

  - Invite a fellow remodeler to discuss systems and suggest solutions to common problems.

☞ Create a task force of your personnel and perhaps a sub to examine, research and solve a particular problem the company is having.

☞ Send employees to trade conventions and to outside seminars. Not only do they learn, they are flattered the company invested in them, and they come back refreshed and reinvigorated with some new ideas.

☞ Send your employee to another remodeler's operation to spend a day and learn how they handle their work. Then host their employee for a day.

☞ Consider certification programs for your employees. They are sponsored by associations and run the gamut from Lead Carpenter Certification to Bath Design Certification. All involve very pertinent learning and testing.

The Value of Positive Feedback

A college professor used to teach seminar-goers an important lesson with the following game. First he would send a volunteer out of the seminar room. Then he would ask another volunteer to hide a coin in a very tough hiding place—often between the pages of a book sitting on a table. The teacher would then call the first volunteer back into the room and ask him/her to find the hidden coin. Each time the volunteer moved toward the coin, the professor would ring a little bell— positive reinforcement. If they moved away from the coin, there would be no sound. With these clues, the searcher could usually find the coin very quickly.

Then the professor would change the rules. Another volunteer was sent from the room and a coin hidden. But this time the searcher would get no clue if they moved toward the coin but they would get a light hit on the arm with a rolled up newspaper if they went in the wrong direction—negative reinforcement. Usually the volunteer would end the game just standing still so they wouldn't be hit and they would abandon the search. What this professor was teaching was the relative value of positive reinforcement versus negative reinforcement.

All of us—owners, employees, subs, suppliers—want feedback on how we are doing. Repeated studies have shown, however, that positive feedback like praise and recognition is many times more powerful in changing behavior than negative feedback like criticism and scolding.

Most remodelers have a "punchlist" approach to coaching their staff. That is, they look for what's wrong and point it out. Instead, get a real edge on your competition by using sincere positive feedback constantly and you'll have well-trained and loyal employees who work hard to get that addictive praising.

Whether you make feedback formal—such as semi-annual performance review—or keep it informal, do make it an integral part of how your company functions. You want feedback from your employees, your clients, your subs and suppliers. Your employees need feedback as an integral part of their growth in your company.

🔔 COACHING TIP

As owner, you need feedback from your employees. Remodeler Bill Weidmann, Weidmann & Associates, Alpharetta, GA, recommends the Stop-Start-Continue method for getting feedback on your performance as company owner, by asking employees

- What they would like you to *stop* doing?
- What they would like you to *start* doing?
- What they would like you to *continue* doing?

VOICES OF EXPERIENCE...

Jack and Pat Tenhulzen, co-owners of Tenhulzen Remodeling in Redmond, WA, use anonymous employee questionnaires to obtain honest feedback on such issues as -

> What do you like most about your job? What do you like least?

> What do you like best about the company?

> Do you feel encouraged to make suggestions for company improvement?

> Are you continually challenged in your job?

> What changes would you make if you were president of this company?

The Tenhulzens say that "If a company is to grow and be successful...it must regard the staff as its most valuable advisors."

REMODELING magazine, May, 1997

Employee Resignations

When a marginal employee resigns, he/she may simply be getting out before being fired. When a valued employee resigns, it can be a blow to the whole company. Fellow workers may wonder if better jobs or higher salaries are available for them elsewhere. Why not find out the real reason or reasons the person is leaving?

The departing employee is able to give you important feedback. Set up an exit interview and ask:

◄ What did you like and not like about the company? (Obtaining a response to the negative portion of this question may take some encouragement.)

— What did you find especially difficult?

— Why are you leaving—better job offer, better pay, dissatisfaction with the present job?

— What changes would you recommend for your position?

In some companies such a resignation is followed by management's "bad mouthing" of the employee. Such unprofessional behavior should be avoided. It creates insecurity among the remaining workers, and it is detrimental to company morale.

Discharging When Necessary

Firing an employee is one of the most difficult tasks any remodeler faces, so many simply delay the inevitable. This delay creates a morale problem with fellow workers and drains profit from the company.

Instead, discover whether the employee lacks the knowledge necessary to do the job, has an attitude problem, is misfitted to the job, or is suffering from some personal crisis. If it's a lack of knowledge, you can decide whether training will improve the worker. An attitude problem on the other hand, can be extremely difficult to improve.

All workers in a remodeling firm are affected by the competence or lack of it in any individual worker. Accepting poor quality or marginal work from one employee is not fair to other workers, and it may cause them to hold back on productivity. You should:

O Move quickly and decisively in this instance. Take action.

O Be sure you have a well-documented record of the employee's infractions.

O Follow the local laws regarding the firing of employees.

☞ COACHING TIP

Attitude problems are tough—maybe even impossible—to change. If this is the problem, consider "freeing up their future" and let them go. Let them go even if their ability to do the job is fine. They are bad apples in the barrel and create stress on everyone. They are working against the positive attitudes you are trying to develop in all your employees. Attitude problems are so tough, it's unlikely you will live long enough to change them.

Make Personnel Your Key to Success

When you hire carefully, train well, and motivate effectively, the impact on productivity, profitability, and customer satisfaction will be enormous. Your people assets will give you a tremendous edge on your competitors. David Gerstel, author of *The Builder's Guide to Running a Successful Construction Company,* (The Taunton Press, Newtown, CT, 1991) sums up this chapter when he says "Good entrepreneurs don't exploit people in an attempt to fatten profits. Take care of the people you work with. They will take care of you."

HOW TO DEVELOP A SUPERSTAR TEAM

★ Consider all employees key employees.

★ Hire people who know more about their specialty than you do.

★ Hire people who can grow with the company.

★ When in doubt, hire the person who wants the job most.

★ Be sure employees know what is expected of them.

★ Base company pay on merit, not seniority.

★ Figure out how to pay employees more than other employers do.

★ Tie pay to productivity and performance.

★ Keep employees informed.

★ Be sure every employee understands how the entire company works and how his/her job fits into that mission.

★ Stress praise. Develop inexpensive prizes, awards, and bonuses to keep motivation high.

★ Challenge employees. Give them as much responsibility as they are ready for. Allow them to fail as well as succeed.

★ Watch the stress level. No employee should have to suffer burnout on the job.

★ Develop simple but effective training programs to keep all employees moving up the ladder.

★ Delegate, rather than direct. Agree on the goal, but let the employee have increasing input on how that goal is to be achieved.

★ Get all employees vitally interested in job costs, annual sales volume goals, and budgets.

★ Be a great coach. Remodeling is a team activity.

5

▪ ▪

Planning for Profit

We have a book in our library called *Do What You Love, the Money Will Follow*. It's a wonderful concept but it simply doesn't fit with our experiences. Those experiences with thousands of remodelers who love what they do, clearly show that you must actively plan for and fight for money —or it will elude you.

This is a very difficult business in which to make consistent profit. Let's start by defining just what profit is:

Profit is the return received on a business undertaking after all operating expenses are met. Those operating expenses include the owner's salary when the owner works day-to-day in the business (as do most remodelers).

It is the role and duty of every business to produce a profit. That extra money remaining at the end of your business year allows you to invest for the business' and the employees' future, save for an economic downturn when you will have to fund the company, share profits with your staff, increase your personal salary, buy an office building, invest in diversified businesses, or pay a disabled employee while he/she recuperates. Profit is good and necessary for a business to be healthy.

Assuring Profitability

Make a commitment to becoming an educated financial manager. Here are some important steps in that decision:

1. Learn the financial facts of your industry by -

   ■ Reading books like this one

   ■ Reading professional remodeling magazines

   ■ Networking with other remodelers

   ■ Attending seminars

   ■ Joining and participating in professional remodeling associations

2. Become one of the top 5% of the industry (in knowledge and sophistication—not necessarily volume) since there is a 95% failure rate for remodelers in the first five years of their businesses.

3. Recognize that in remodeling you will make your profit by planning, not doing—by using a pencil, not a hammer.

4. Operate on the premise that profit—not volume—represents business growth. A remodeler cannot lose money on every job and make it up in volume.

5. Have enough capital to bridge difficult financial times. Many remodelers have no additional funds and simply ride on the cash flow surf until it crashes. Build a contingency fund for your company as quickly as you can.

6. Plan for profit with a budget. View financial planning as liberating—not as restrictive. A plan that provides a roadmap to profitability can be comforting and will provide an early warning system if you are slipping.

7. View budgeting as a tool to test various profit scenarios and create "what ifs." Making a plan for profit nearly

always involves altering some of the factors such as volume, personnel or new office space. It invariably means running the business differently from the way it would have been run if no plan had been made.

8. Plan for a 10% net profit (after the owner's salary is accounted for in job costs or in overhead). If the required markup seems to make the jobs difficult to sell, learn to market and sell more effectively—but do not lower the required price.

9. Make every employee responsible for profit. Employees need to share your goals and agree on the means to achieve those goals. You may need to be more open with employees on financial matters than you have been in the past.

10. Learn that overhead as a percentage of volume usually goes up as remodeling firms get larger. Also, larger average job sizes usually lower the percentage of overhead, while small jobs need proportionately more overhead.

11. Focus on required *gross profit* (dollars and percentage) as defined by the budget as the key number the company must achieve to be successful. Whoever sells can be sure the appropriate gross profit is built in to the sales price. Whoever supervises production can focus on bringing in jobs on budget so that they produce the correct gross profit.

Don't be the average remodeler who believes that fine craftsmanship will lead directly to a great bottom line. Don't be the remodeler who learns about the financial performance of the company (inevitably a disappointment) only during April of the following year. Don't be the remodeler who never gets job cost reports because they're just too much work to generate.

All those remodelers will be gone within a few years. Commit to being the financial planner and manager of your company. Commit to frequent reporting that tells you how you are doing and gives you time to make changes if you are getting off track.

Here's what you need to do to be a savvy financial manager:

◀ First, manage your cash flow.

◀ Secondly, plan your profit (budget) so you know exactly what you need to do.

◀ Thirdly, track your progress against that plan with job costs, profit and loss reports and balance sheets so that you can see where the company is going and take action to avert problems and maximize profit.

Healthy Cash Flow

Where does cash flow fit in the picture? Cash flow is the visible money flowing in and out of your checking account. Many remodelers feel flush when there's money in the account and broke when it's empty. Positive cash flow is very important to all businesses and you do want to monitor it. But it is different from profitability. Let's review cash flow before we move on to making your company profitable.

There are three rules to having a healthy cash flow:

○ Collect money early.

○ Pay money out as late as you can without damaging your credit.

○ And be profitable so more money comes in than goes out.

One of the great financial benefits of remodeling—one that would turn businesspeople in other fields green with envy—is that the remodeler can run ahead of his/her client financially because you are able to collect now for work you're planning to do soon. If you work these rules of cash flow well, you could be running on $20,000, $30,000 or $40,000 of your client's money. That allows you to run your business with OPM—Other Peoples' Money. However, this does not give a remodeler license to pay old bills with new money!

Following the three golden rules of cash flow, here are 15 tried and true tips for creating favorable cash flow in your business—assuming you are also profitable! They fall under 4 categories:

1. optimizing contract draws
2. collecting smartly
3. buying carefully
4. excelling as a money manager

Optimize Contract Draws

1. If you are using draws based on job progress, always word those draws to become due upon *start of* a phase rather than *completion of,* and you will maximize your cash and minimize your arguments with the customer. For instance, you can substitute "upon start of trim" for "upon completion of drywall." You are simply trying to make the draws less open to interpretation.

2. Collect a first draw that is fair to the buyer but gives you as much leverage as possible. Review state law. Often remodelers ask for 20-30% down with mid-size jobs, 50% with small jobs. If the job is particularly material-heavy, consider a larger first draw. In kitchen remodeling, remodelers will typically collect 50% of the contract before commencement to compensate for the large volume of special materials that must be ordered.

3. Split the final draw into two smaller draws—the first is substantial completion (when the space is ready for occupancy) and a smaller draw upon completion of the punchlist. Don't

let other charges like change orders, selections and time and material charges fall into the final draws. Be sure to bill them as early as possible.

4. Some remodelers collect draws based on a time period. They may collect every week or every two weeks. If the Basehart job is a $12,000 job and is expected to take six weeks, the remodeler will collect $2,000 a week. If there is a delay, the draw schedule will be adjusted. This type of draw is very helpful for foreseeing incoming cash flow.

5. An increasing number of remodelers who work on a *cost plus* or *time and materials* basis are requesting a substantial "retainer" before they begin the job and are drawing against that retainer which is very helpful for cash flow.

Be a Smart Collector

6. Hand deliver invoices and personally pick up checks. Over a year's period, this practice will make major inroads on cash flow problems.

7. Make bill collecting a person-to-person effort. Do not just make and send additional invoices. Phone, discuss, and meet the customer in person to settle any confusion, questions or problems quickly.

8. When your client is another business such as a commercial property owner or insurance company, find out who will approve bills and pay them—and ask about the firm's payment procedures. Several offices may have to approve an invoice before it is paid. An invoice may need two or three signatures. Knowing the system allows the remodeler to expedite payment. Faxing two invoices may help: one for the person supervising construction and one for the person actually approving payments. Find out the client's preferred system and work within it to obtain prompt payment.

Be a Foxy Buyer

9. Always pay bills in time to take any discount offered for early payment. That percentage you save for spending your money 20 days earlier is a bargain. Do it. Pay other bills on the last date that will maintain the firm's good credit.

10. Subcontract rather than employ when possible. Subcontractors are often paid only one or two times during a job whereas your own labor may be paid each week.

11. Rather than purchasing in cash or on account, consider using credit cards that give you a rebate or airline mileage where possible. With some credit cards the purchases are interest free if the balance is paid in total each month. Also, using a credit card also allows you to delay payment for a month or more. However, don't let this get out of hand and get you into debt. These fifteen tips are meant to smooth cash flow—not tempt you into deep indebtedness.

12. If you do not have supplier accounts now, see if you are eligible for them. A monthly account may save you money both through the extended credit and through the available discounts.

Excel as a Money Manager

13. Consider bi-weekly payroll. You'll increase your cash float while cutting the cost of doing payroll in half. Thousands of remodelers have accomplished this successfully and, yes, field personnel can make the adjustment.

14. As your volume gets larger, you may want to develop a line of credit with a bank that can be used to smooth out the firm's cash needs. Think of a line of credit only as a short term bridge loan to allow you to take work that requires your temporary financing of the job—not to get you out of financial trouble. Clean up—by paying up—your line of credit once a year.

15. Watch warehousing. Does the savings from buying in quantity and stocking frequently used material really surpass the cost of space, of inventorying, and of tracking damage to stored materials? Inventory ties up cash.

Cash flow can be your friend or foe. We've seen remodeling businesses devastated by lack of cash. The owner's focus becomes robbing Peter to pay Paul instead of running an effective business. However, if you are running your company with a loss currently, let us cheer you by telling you that we've seen remodelers make striking comebacks with the help of excellent money management.

Build up some capital in your firm. That will reduce stress more than almost any other act you can take. Remember, cash flow is your friend...but it's not the whole story!

Budgeting—Your Plan for Profit

The majority of remodelers who fail in the first 5 years do so because they neglect to budget their firm's profitability. Budgeting is simply planning for profit and expressing that plan in words and figures.

Most remodelers who fail simply mark up their estimated costs with what they think the prospect will buy and with what they think will at least pay their wages. Unfortunately the costs of running a $200,000 company, a $435,000 company, or a $600,000 company are simply too complex for anyone, no matter how intelligent, to guess at. You must have a plan on paper.

Many remodelers do not plan because they believe they will simply put down on paper the plan that is already in their heads. Anyone who has prepared a budget can testify that that just is not so. Budgeting always involves changes to the original plan. The first budget frequently shows no profit for the year's work. It must be reworked. Perhaps a few percentage points are added to markup, the purchase of a new truck is put off for another year, or the remodeler makes a commitment to save 5 percent in job costs, etc.

☞ COACHING TIP

As consultants we often review financial statements that show the remodeler has worked an entire year only to show a loss. It's not uncommon to find that that loss was predictable from the beginning had they only done a budget. Budgeting lets you try out your financial formula before you work 365 days with no plan or a plan that simply doesn't work.

Budgeting on paper will convince you just how hard it is to get a 10 percent net profit and how easy it would be to blow that 10% with impulsive spending or job costs that overrun. Budgeting will show you the difficulty of reducing overhead without laying off people. Budgeting demonstrates that money saved in efficient operation goes directly to the bottom line.

Profit planning is the most important task a remodeler will do all year. Budgeting or planning for profit for a remodeling firm involves detailing the costs of running your company for the year. We know that you know how to estimate jobs so we also know you can easily estimate your company costs. Here are the five key steps:

1. **Decide the net profit** you want and deserve over and above your salary.

2. **Decide the volume** of work you can realistically anticipate producing.

3. Estimate your overhead costs for producing that level of work.

4. Use the PROFITFIRST SYSTEM© to play out various scenarios (see page 84).

5. Develop the final budget that you will use for the year.

Budgeting Step 1: Decide Your Net Profit

Planning for net profit—money left after your job costs and overhead expenses are paid—is one of the most important budgeting steps. Without this 8-10 percent of volume needed to stay in business, a remodeling firm will not last long. Net profit pays the remodeler for risk-taking (and remodeling is a risky business). Profit also provides savings for the business in case of hard times. Net profit provides the seed money to invest in the future growth of the company.

Every remodeling company should build an interest bearing contingency fund equal to 4 to 7% of gross sales volume. This is available to use to fund future growth, unforeseen catastrophes, to diversify, or to bridge cash flow problems.

☞ COACHING TIP

Plan for your net profit of 10%. The actual net often drops to 5 to 8 percent during the year—usually because of job cost overruns, lower than predicted volume, or higher than predicted overhead. If you plan for less than 10%, it will inevitably erode to zero (breakeven) or a loss. Unfortunately, many businesses work at the break-even point. An entire year's work leaves nothing at the end of that year to fuel growth or stability. Even more dangerous is the fact that the business is vulnerable to bankruptcy because it has no contingency fund.

Budgeting Step 2: Decide on the Volume of Work

Planning for profit means putting down on paper a careful guesstimate of the amount of work the company will do the next year. This volume number is not what will be sold but the volume of work that will be completed by production in that year. A large job sold in December might not be completed until February so only part of this job would be counted in the year it was sold. The remodeler needs to consider both the company's capability and the economy of the city or town in order to arrive at a reasonable volume.

Budgeting Step 3: Estimate Your Overhead Costs

Now it's time to determine the yearly overhead for your company including all expenses not reported as direct job costs. Overhead includes items like rent, utilities, office manager salary, liability insurance, marketing expenses, legal and accounting fees and your salary if you are not included in job costs. It's not uncommon for overhead to run 20-35% of volume in a remodeling company.

☞ COACHING TIP

Decide exactly what items you will include in direct job costs. Everyone agrees that labor, material and subs used on the job should be included. Most experts feel the labor burden (Workers Compensation insurance, employer's Social Security contribution, state and federal unemployment tax on field employees) should be a part of direct job costs. Some remodelers include their production manager and sales commissions in job costs. The key point we want to make is to decide and then be consistent in including all those costs in your estimate (before you mark up), in your budget, in your profit and loss statements and actual job cost reports.

Budgeting Step 4:
Planning with the Seven Step ProfitFirst System©:

To make this simple budgeting shortcut work for you, all you have to do is to supply three critical numbers: net profit, volume, and overhead. This format allows you to run a number of scenarios very quickly to see what your across-the-board markup will have to be to achieve your profit goals. Then when you find the combination you like, prepare a full formal budget.

1. Determine your desired **net profit**. As owner/investor what should my return be? What return could I get elsewhere? What are my risks?
   Desired Net Profit $ _____

2. Calculate a reasonable **sales/production volume** for the year.
   Sales/Production Volume Goal $_____

3. List your **overhead costs** to produce the above volume. (Include your salary if you are not a direct job cost)
   Overhead Costs $_____

4. How much **gross profit** will I need?
   (Answer 1 + Answer 3 = Gross Profit)
   Gross Profit Needed $_____

5. What should my **job costs** run in dollars?
   (Answer 2 - Answer 4 = job costs in dollars)
   Job Costs in Dollars $_____

6. What should my **job costs** run in percentages?
   (Answer 5 ÷ Answer 2 = job costs in percentages)
   Job Cost Percentage _____%

7. What will my **markup** be on jobs if I use an across-the-board markup? (1 ÷ percentage shown in Answer 6)
   Markup Percentage _____%

Putting the PROFITFIRST SYSTEM© to Work

Example 1: Joe is planning for his next business year. He is committed to achieving a net profit of $25,000. He's planning to sell and produce a volume of $300,000 and his overhead runs $65,000. He wants to use an across-the-board markup on all job costs. Let's figure out what markup Joe will need to use to achieve his goals.

1. Net Profit	$ 25,000
2. Volume	$300,000
3. Overhead	$ 65,000
4. Gross Profit	$ 90,000
5. Job costs in dollars	$210,000
6. Job costs in percentage	70%
7. Markup	1.42

(Joe would multiply his job costs by 1.42 to get his selling price. Thus a job with $100 in costs would sell for $142.)

Example 2: How will the planning change if Joe wants $35,000 net profit? It's your turn. Check your answer at the bottom.

1. Net Profit $_____

2. Volume $_____

3. Overhead $_____

4. Gross Profit $_____

5. Job costs in dollars $_____

6. Job costs in percentage _____%

7. Markup _____%

Example 3: Joe decides that he will be able to produce $400,000 in volume which will add $7,000 to his overhead. He is satisfied to keep his net profit at $25,000. Now what markup must he use?

1. Net Profit $ _____

2. Volume $_____

3. Overhead $ _____

4. Gross Profit $_____

5. Job costs in dollars $_____

6. Job costs in percentage _____%

7. Markup _____%

ANSWERS—

Example 2: Joe will need a markup of 1.5 on his job costs.

Example 3: Joe will need a markup of 1.32 on his job costs.

LESSON 1: <u>You</u> are in charge of your markup. Don't take anyone else's markup. Remember, PROFITFIRST!©

LESSON 2: Focus on the Gross Profit needed. Everything else is just a means to an end. We call that "bringing home the gross profit bacon!"

AN ACTUAL BUDGET

Revenue/Income		$1,350,000.00	
DIRECT JOB COSTS			
Materials		273,000.00	
Subcontractors		492,000.00	
Labor		45,000.00	
	Subtotal	810,000.00	60.00%
VARIABLE JOB COSTS			
Production Manager		47,000.00	
Tools & Equipment		1,500.00	
Auto Expense		6,800.00	
Permits		5,000.00	
Phones & Beepers		3,200.00	
	Subtotal	63,300.00	4.69%
Total Job Costs		873,300.00	64.69%
Gross Profit		476,700.00	35.31%
GENERAL & ADMINISTRATIVE			
Owners Salary		62,400.00	
Salaries-Office		7,000.00	
Amortization of leasehold improvements		1,100.00	
Collection expense		1,250.00	
Consulting fees		400.00	
Conventions & Seminars		5,000.00	
Depreciation		7,500.00	
Directors fees		2,500.00	
Donations		100.00	
Computer Maintenance		700.00	
Computer Hardware & Software		1,500.00	
Dues & Subscriptions		5,000.00	
Electricity		400.00	
Heat		500.00	
Insurance-disability		1,500.00	
Insurance-general		14,200.00	

Insurance-health	15,000.00	
Insurance-keyman life	300.00	
Licenses	100.00	
Meetings-subs, employees and awards	1,700.00	
Office cleaning	1,000.00	
Office remodeling, repairs & maintenance	6,000.00	
Office supplies & expense	10,000.00	
Postage	2,500.00	
Rent	11,200.00	
Taxes-social Security	20,000.00	
Taxes-federal unemployment	400.00	
Taxes-state unemployment	200.00	
Taxes-personal property	600.00	
Telephone	4,500.00	
Telephone answering service	1,200.00	
Total General & Administrative	**241,850.00**	**17.91%**
SELLING EXPENSES		
Salaries-sales	42,000.00	
Advertising-Newspapers	5,500.00	
Advertising-Yellow & White Pages	5,500.00	
Automobile expense	11,800.00	
Bad Debts	4,000.00	
Depreciation	4,700.00	
Entertainment	1,000.00	
Sales Promotion-shows & tours	13,000.00	
Image, job site marketing & referrals	15,000.00	
Phones & Beepers	3,200.00	
Total Selling Expenses	**105,700.00**	**7.83%**
Total General Administrative & Selling Expense	**347,550.00**	**25.74%**
NET INCOME	**129,150.00**	**9.57%**

Calculating Your Break-Even Point

Your break-even point is the amount of sales/completions needed to pay all the bills and leave the company solvent—but with no net profit. To find your break-even point, divide your overhead dollars by the percent of planned gross profit.

$$\text{Break-even} = \frac{\text{overhead \$}}{\text{gross profit \%}}$$

In the sample budget the overhead is $347,550 and the planned gross profit percentage is 35%. Dividing the overhead by .35 shows that this company will break even (pay all bills but make no profit) if they produce $993,000 in work at the 35% gross profit. If their gross profit were to drop to 29%, they would need to produce nearly 1.2 million in volume.

You can see that no profit is made in a company until the breakeven point is reached. After that, all gross profit goes to net profit.

The second lesson here is that when your gross profit erodes even a few percentage points, it has a disastrous effect on your planning and profitability.

Marking Up to Make Money: What Method Is Best for You?

Budgeting leads directly to the question "What will my markup be?" The costs of the job must be marked up enough to create a sales price that will produce the gross profit to cover your budgeted overhead and net profit. The most common way to develop a sales price in remodeling is with an *across-the-board* markup on job costs. For example, if your markup is 1.42, then all jobs receive that markup. Or you may do commercial and residential work and mark up commercial 1.35 and residential 1.45. This is the markup method that is most commonly taught and used because it makes planning very simple and lets you know exactly what volume will produce the gross profit you need.

Using an Across-the-Board Markup

TO ACHIEVE THIS GROSS PROFIT	MARK UP COST BY THIS PERCENTAGE	JOB COST EXPECTED TO RUN
25.0	33.3	75%*
26.0	35.0	
27.0	37.0	
28.0	39.0	
28.5	40.0	
29.0	40.9	
30.0	43.0	
31.0	45.0	
32.0	47.0	
33.0	49.0	
33.5	50.0	66.5%
34.0	51.0	
35.0	54.0	
36.0	56.0	PROFESSIONAL
37.5	60.0	LEVEL OF
38.0	61.0	OPERATION
39.0	64.0	
40.0	66.7	60.0%
42.6	75.0	
45.0	82.0	
50.0	100.0	
66.7	200.0	
75.0	300.0	25%

* To fill in the Job Cost column, simply subtract Gross Profit from 100% (100% – 25%=75%)

However, there is never only one way to do anything! Here are some alternate methods for developing your sales price and their practitioners swear by them.

1. Differential markup: Labor, material and subs are each marked up with a different percentage. Usually labor is very heavily burdened with gross profit.

> Let's say Joe, who had to mark up up his jobs 1.43 in the PROFITFIRST$^{©}$ across-the-board markup example, decides to use a differential markup. His labor on $300,000 in work runs $65,000 and he marks it up 2.0 = $130,000, his subs run $70,000 and he marks them up 1.3 = 91,000, his materials run $70,000 and he applies a 1.1 markup = $77,000, giving him a total volume of $298,000 and a gross profit of $93,000.

This system will make Joe more expensive on heavy labor jobs and less expensive on light labor jobs. Many remodelers who choose this method favor light labor jobs and also feel that labor should carry the brunt of gross profit.

2. Labor-based markup: In this system the remodeler totals the number of hours available to sell in the year. They then take their projected gross profit and divide by that number of hours and find out how much gross profit each hour must produce. The labor hours in the estimate then are marked up with this additional sum.

> Joe has 6,000 labor hours to sell in a year and needs to obtain $90,000 in gross profit. Each hour of labor must be marked up to carry $15 of overhead—6,000 x $15 = $90,000. Joe's best carpenter Hal earns $18 an hour and Joe pays an additional $6 in burden for each hour Hal works. When Joe does an estimate, he charges $18 + $6 + $15(markup) = $39 an hour for Hal's time.

3. Schedule-based markup. In this system the gross profit is divided by the number of working days and then by the number of crews the company will run for the year. Each job must be marked up by the number of days needed to complete the job times the gross profit per day. This type of markup definitely focuses remodelers on producing the right amount of gross profit each day and being sure that jobs do not run over the schedule.

> Joe's company has 250 working days in which to generate $90,000 of gross profit. Each working day must produce $360 in gross profit (250 x 360 = $90,000) Joe runs one job at a time. The Harris job will take 4 weeks or 20 working days x $360 = $7,200. Therefore its costs will be marked up by adding $7,200 to the anticipated job costs.

4. Flexible markup: Many remodelers will decide how much markup should be applied on a job-by-job basis, based on the type of job, how the year is going, need for the company to get the job, and the level of other prospective jobs. You must have a firm handle on your budget to use this method and still end up with the required gross profit at the end of the year.

COACHING TIP

The across-the-board markup system makes forecasting gross profit very easy. However, if you use a different markup system, you still need to make careful forecasts of how your gross profit will be generated.

The across-the-board markup is the easiest. The others work but call for more sophistication in their application. Choose your markup method. Make sure it can be monitored at least monthly. And make sure it brings home the gross profit bacon!

Develop a <u>Monthly</u> Budget

Once an annual budget or profit plan is done, it can be divided into a monthly budget against which actual expenditures can be compared. Don't simply divide the annual plan by 12. While some expenditures such as rent fall neatly into 12 divisions, other expenditures like insurance premiums may be paid as a lump sum one or two times a year.

Most remodelers find their business to be cyclical. For instance, a deck builder may find the winter months to be really slow, spring and fall to be the highest volume months, and summer to be relatively weak. Thus, it's best to make your budget cyclical so that accurate comparisons to actual expenses can be made. That way you'll plan for those items in the appropriate month and have a much better feel for your cash flow needs throughout the year.

ANNUAL BUDGET DIVIDED INTO A MONTHLY BUDGET

In the following remodeler's budget (we're showing you just page three of it) some of expenses have simply been divided by twelve and others are shown in the month they are to be paid. You'll notice the number of weeks per month listed above so that payroll costs can be allotted accurately to the proper month. If you pay weekly, you'll have 5 pay periods some months and 4 in others. Be sure to start your budget with income goals as they also are cyclical.

ANNUAL BUDGET TURNED INTO A MONTHLY BUDGET (partial)

DESCRIPTION	Total	Jan	February	March	April	May
Weeks per month	52	4	4	4	5	4
Legal & Accounting	$ 2,700	$225	$225	$225	$225	$225
Tax return preparation	0					
Accounting Services	0					
Legal Fees	0					
Office Expense	25,200	2,100	2,100	2,100	2,100	2,100
Postage Meter & Scale	580		145			145
Equipment Repair/Main	0					
Copier Svc Contract	816		204			204
Laser Printer	480	40	40	40	40	40
Fax machine	180	15	15	15	15	15
Other Equip Repairs	0					
Computer	0					
Maintenance	600	50	50	50	50	50
Software Support	1,605	1,605				
Capital Stock tax	392			98		
Outside Services	2,280	570			570	
Payroll Tax/FICA	30,000	2,500	2,500	2,500	2,500	2,500
Federal Unemploy Tax	1,840	930	300	300	150	20
PA Unemploy Tax	3,000	800	800	500	100	100
Penalties	1,412			353		
Postage	3,624	302	302	302	302	302
Rent - Shop	4,800	400	400	400	400	400
Rent - Office	19,000	750	750	750	750	2,000
Repairs & Maint-Equip	1,740	145	145	145	145	145
Repairs & Maint-Bldg	0					
Depreciation	0					
Salaries-Office	86,568	6,659	6,659	6,659	6,659	9,989
Other Salaries	48,000	4,000	4,000	4,000	4,000	4,000
Stockholder Salary	78,000	6,000	6,000	6,000	6,000	9,000
Office Supplies	720	60	60	60	60	60
Telephone-Office	3,060	255	255	255	255	255
Telephone-Cellular	3,120	260	260	260	260	260

Dennis Gehman, GEHMAN CUSTOM BUILDER Inc., Telford, PA

June	July	August	September	October	November	December
4	5	4	5	4	4	5
$225	$225	$225	$225	$225	$225	$225
2,100	2,100	2,100	2,100	2,100	2,100	2,100
		145			145	
		204			204	
40	40	40	40	40	40	40
15	15	15	15	15	15	15
50	50	50	50	50	50	50
98			98			98
	570			570		
2,500	2,500	2,500	2,500	2,500	2,500	2,500
20	20	20	20	20	20	20
100	100	100	100	100	100	100
353			353			353
302	302	302	302	302	302	302
400	400	400	400	400	400	400
2,000	2,000	2,000	2,000	2,000	2,000	2,000
145	145	145	145	145	145	145
6,659	6,659	6,659	6,659	9,989	6,659	6,659
4,000	4,000	4,000	4,000	4,000	4,000	4,000
6,000	6,000	6,000	6,000	9,000	6,000	6,000
60	60	60	60	60	60	60
255	255	255	255	255	255	255
260	260	260	260	260	260	260

Reassess Your Profit Plan Quarterly

View your budget as a flexible instrument because in the fast moving remodeling business, plans change and sales change. You may decide to hire a new office person, insurance or rent may go up, and beepers may be needed. A regularly scheduled quarterly update and review allows you to recheck company profitability based on current information.

Your Financial Planning is Now in Order

You've done your homework and prepared plans for how you will make a profit in the next year. This planning includes these three elements:

- ◎ Your company budget.
- ◎ Your markup method.
- ◎ Your individual job estimates (discussed in a later chapter) which budget each job.

Now let's look at how you can track your progress against your goals and make sure you stay on track.

6

Monitoring Your Financial Progress Against the Plan

Developing the best plan for profit won't help if you don't keep track of how you are doing against that plan and make corrections when you deviate. Much of accounting and bookkeeping is meant to help you monitor profit and expense. Never think for a moment that financial reports are only for the government to use in taxing. Financial reports are—first and foremost—for you to use to manage your company intelligently. Let's look at the reports that help you monitor your progress.

THE PLAN	MONITORING YOUR PROGRESS	HOW OFTEN?
Budget	Profit & Loss Report	monthly
Job Estimate	Actual Job Cost Report	at least monthly

The Profit and Loss Report

The *Profit and Loss Report* or *Operating Statement* summarizes just how your company has performed for the past month, quarter or year. If properly formatted, this report tells you how much income you had, and what your expenses were (in job cost and overhead categories) and what remained as net profit. Each year you begin with a fresh slate in this report—nothing is carried over from the previous year in income or expense.

THE PROFIT & LOSS STATEMENT SIMPLY PUT...

Income – Job Costs = Gross Profit
Gross Profit – Overhead = Net Profit

Linda W. Case, THE REMODELER'S GUIDE TO MAKING AND MANAGING MONEY, 1996.

THE P & L WITH A LITTLE MORE DETAIL

Your *Profit and Loss Report* tells a story—the story of your business over a period of time. Here's an example:

Craftsman Remodelers specializes in repairs. Over the past three months, they've been paid $24,300 by their customers to do a large number of repairs. To do those repairs it took $8,495 in payroll costs, $4,900 in materials and $2,400 in electrical, plumbing, hvac and tile subcontractor costs.

Even after Craftsman has paid all of the above costs, they have to pay $6,305 in overhead costs for the three months. If anything is left, it is profit. The owner is paid in job costs.

THE P & L REPORT:	3 Months
Income	$24,300
Job Costs	
Labor	8,495
Material	4,900
Subs	2,400
Gross Profit	$ 8,505
Overhead	6,305
Net Profit	2,200

Linda W. Case, THE REMODELER'S GUIDE TO MAKING AND MANAGING MONEY, 1996.

P & L Guidelines

Here are some guidelines for reading your P & L Report effectively:

—◄ Remember, the P & L Report is a management document for your use. Be sure it's formatted so you can understand it and use the valuable information it contains.

—◄ Get comfortable with your P & L. It is like a job cost report (see later chapter on job costing)—but for the whole company. Understand it well enough to be able to explain it to another person.

—◄ Insist that you receive your reports within two weeks of the month end. Two weeks is a reasonable amount of time for the bookkeeper to prepare the report and yet it gives you timely information.

—◄ Be sure to include percentages in a right hand column for ease of reading. These percentages are what you should be focusing on as you scan your report.

—◄ Be sure the expense categories are properly sorted. In particular, be sure that only items included in your job estimates as job costs are included in your P & L as job costs.

—◄ Be sure to include labor burden and benefits in job costs so that both light labor and heavy labor jobs are accurately priced and so that you won't get caught holding the bag in your workers comp audit.

—◄ Zero in on the projected job cost percentage based on your markup. For instance, if you mark up 50%, you are anticipating a 33% gross profit and 67% job cost. Job costs that run too high are the most common problem area for remodelers. Be aggressive about solving it!

◄ Watch that all of your individual job cost reports totalled together equal your job costs on your P & L statement.

◄ Always put your owner's salary in your P & L as a cost of doing business. You might sort your salary into job costs if you work on the job or if you are production manager and that is considered a job cost in your company. Or you may put your owner's salary in overhead if you sell or administer. Do not take your base salary from the bottom line net profit.

◄ Be sure to include depreciation (on equipment, vehicles, etc.) in your P & L as a line item overhead expense each month. Ask your accountant how much it should be. Since your end-of-year report will contain this, you should get accustomed to seeing it as a reduction on your normal monthly report.

◄ If you have two diversified types of businesses (perhaps custom home building and remodeling or replacement windows and design/build remodeling) report income and expense separately for each branch of your company (even though you keep them on the same P & L report.) That way you can analyze income, job costs, gross profit for each segment separately and make informed decisions as to whether to grow, maintain or reduce certain parts of your business.

◄ One of the most valuable analyses of your P & L is to compare it to the budget for the time period (see Chapter 5 on Budgeting). Your budget creates a roadmap to profit and your P & L shows how you are doing in staying on that roadmap. By analyzing this monthly, you are able to take quick action when you see the company going off track in some area.

P & L Showing Budget to Actual Comparison

This report—from an actual remodeler—contrasts a six month P & L total with the budget totals projected for that six month period. The Net Income actually ran $10,000 higher than budgeted.

Budget to Actual Comparison
Income Statement
6 months

	Current Balance	Current Percent	Budget	Budget Percent	Dollar Variance
Commercial Operations Income	$ 38,079.80	7.32 %	$ 9,999.96	2.00 %	$ (28,079.84)
Residential Operations Income	475,494.25	91.35	484,999.98	96.84	9,505.73
Design Services Income	6,328.03	1.22	4,999.98	1.00	(1,328.05)
Trade Discounts	586.73	.11	799.98	.16	213.25
TOTAL INCOME	**$ 520,488.81**	**100.00%**	**$500,799.90**	**100%**	**(19,688.91)**
DIRECT COSTS					
Direct Materials	$ 75,606.13	14.53%	90,000.00	17.97%	$ 14,393.87
Subcontractor Costs	207,685.61	39.90	167,499.96	33.45	(40,185.65)
Direct Labor	32,762.74	6.29	33,003.96	6.59	241.22
Tool Rental Allowance	49.50	.01	500.00	.10	450.50
Direct Labor Vehicle Allowance	960.00	.19	960.00	.19	0.00
Prod. Vac/Holiday Pay	1,356.00	.26	1,596.00	.32	240.00
Prod. FICA-ER	2,694.49	.51	2,725.98	.54	31.49
Prod. FUTA	165.54	.04	264.00	.06	98.46
Prod. SUTA	448.87	.08	280.98	.05	(167.89)
Prod. Workers Comp.	4,394.82	.85	5,604.00	1.12	1,209.18
Production Vehicle Fuel	1,053.64	.20	980.00	.20	(73.64)
Prod. Vehicle Maint/Repair	636.72	.12	679.96	.13	43.24
Equipment Rentals	637.33	.12	999.96	.20	362.63
Site Utilities	0.00	0.00	49.98	.01	49.98
Site Sanitation/Landfill	2,969.88	.58	3,000.00	.60	30.12
Building Permits	1,644.51	.31	1,500.00	.30	(144.51)
Plans/Design Costs	4,180.26	.80	3,750.00	.75	(430.26)
Gen. Liab. Ins.-Carpenters	2,507.92	.49	1,549.50	.31	(958.42)
Gen. Liab. Ins.-Tools & Equip.	94.01	.01	94.01	.02	0.00
Gen. Liab. Ins.-Subcontractors	1,212.49	.24	1,212.49	.24	0.00

BUDGET TO ACTUAL COMPARISON
INCOME STATEMENT
— 6 months

	Current Balance	Current Percent	Budget	Budget Percent	Dollar Variance
Production Supplies/Materials	838.22	.16	720.00	.14	(118.22)
Prod. Equipment Maint/Repair	0.00-	0.00	99.96	.02	99.96
Other Direct Expenses	122.14	.02	120.00	.03	(2.14)
TOTAL JOB COSTS	**$ 342,020.82**	**65.71%**	**$317,190.74**	**63.34%**	**($24,830.08)**
GROSS PROFIT	**$ 178,467.99**	**34.29%**	**$183,609.16**	**36.66%**	**$5,141.17**
EXPENSES					
Officer Salary	$ 31,000.00	5.96%	$ 31,000.00	6.19%	0
Office Salaries/Wages	18,969.25	3.64	18,661.98	3.72	(307.27)
Office Vacation/Holiday	1,092.75	.21	1,087.98	.22	(4.77)
Office Bonuses	50.00	.01	0.00	0	(50.00)
Prod. Manager Salary	21,600.00	4.15	21,274.98	4.25	(325.02)
Prod. Mgr Vac/Holiday Pay	1,800.00	.35	2,124.96	.42	324.96
Sales/Commissions/Finder Fees	17,080.50	3.28	30,000.00	5.99	12,919.50
Employee Perks/Bonuses	303.30	.06	240.00	.05	(63.30)
Subcontractor Perks/Bonuses	30.00	0.00	300.00	.06	270.00
FICA-ER	6,948.35	1.34	5,346.00	1.07	(1,602.35)
FUTA	202.62	.04	214.00	.04	11.38
SUTA	801.86	.15	812.00	.16	10.14
Workers Comp.	966.66	.19	1,338.96	.27	372.30
Direct Building Expense	12.10	0.00	48.00	.01	35.90
Architect/Design	20.00	0.00	168.00	.03	148.00
Photography	270.33	.05	240.00	.05	(30.33)
Office Veh. Fuel	450.73	.09	412.50	.08	(38.23)
Office Veh. Insurance	227.79	.04	210.00	.05	(17.39)
Office Veh. Maint/Repair	175.23	.04	75.00	.01	(100.23)
Office Veh. Depr.	2,042.16	.39	2,042.10	.41	(.06)
Office Equip. Depr.	1,328.72	.26	1,187.52	.24	(141.20)
General Liability	240.00	.04	240.00	.04	0.00
Accounting	1,150.00	.22	900.00	.18	(250.00)
Advertising	- 0 -	0.00	60.00	.02	60.00
Bank Charges	24.00	.01	96.00	.02	72.00
Charitable Contributions	66.50	.01	180.00	.03	113.50
Communications	4,387.67	.84	3,399.96	.68	(987.71)
Computer Expenses	3,353.34	.65	3,105.00	.62	(248.34)
Dues & Subscriptions	$ 389.95	.07%	54.54	.01	(335.41)
Education	1,973.37	.38	2,439.96	.49	466.59
Group Health Insurance	1,213.28	.24	1,248.00	.25	34.72

BUDGET TO ACTUAL COMPARISON
INCOME STATEMENT
— 6 months

	Current Balance	Current Percent	Budget	Budget Percent	Dollar Variance
Medical Insurance Supplement	900.00	.17	900.00	.18	0.00
Group Disability Insurance	700.45	.13	670.00	.13	(30.45)
Legal	(770.34)	(.15)	600.00	.12	1,370.34
Marketing	2,843.84	.55	4,999.98	1.00	2,156.14
Meals & Entertainment	629.75	.12	600.00	.12	(29.75)
Office Rent	3,600.00	.69	3,600.00	.72	0.00
Office Maint/Repair	262.31	.05	360.00	.07	97.69
Office Supplies	1,214.75	.24	780.00	.16	(434.75)
Office Equipment Maint/Repair	155.35	.03	390.00	.07	234.65
Postage	842.59	.16	390.00	.08	(452.59)
Shop Rent	2,484.00	.48	2,484.00	.50	0.00
Shop Maint/Repair	164.55	.03	300.00	.06	135.45
Small Tools	426.02	.08	499.98	.10	73.96
Tool Maint/Repair	163.95	.03	249.96	.05	86.01
Travel	1,852.97	.36	1,999.98	.40	147.01
Trade Associations	75.00	.01	75.00	.01	0.00
Utilities	1,195.64	.23	1,200.00	.24	4.36
Other Operating Expenses	0.00	0.00	120.00	.02	120.00
Uniforms	577.50	.11	199.98	.04	(377.52)
Other Expenses.	0.00	0.00	300.00	.06	300.00
TOTAL EXPENSES	$ 135,488.39	26.03%	$149,226.32	29.80%	$13,737.93
NET INCOME BEFORE OTHER INCOME	$ 42,979.60	8.26%	$ 34,382.84	6.87%	$ (8,596.76)
Interest Income	$ 898.17	.17%	$ 360.00	.07	$ (538.17)
Brokerage Interest Income	1,797.00	.35	2,040.00	.40	243.00
Dividend Income	5,393.00	1.03	5,393.00	1.08	0.00
Other Income	1,908.19	.37	600.00	.12	(1,308.19)
TOTAL OTHER INCOME	$ 9,996.36	1.92%	$ 8,393.00	1.68	$ (1,603.36)
NET INCOME (LOSS) BEFORE TAXES	$ 52,975.96	10.18%	$42,775.84	8.54	$ (10,200.12)
Income Taxes	2,920.00	.56	2,080.00	.41	(840.00)
NET INCOME (LOSS)	$ 50,055.96	9.62%	$ 40,695.84	8.13%	$ (9,360.12)

Linda W. Case, THE REMODELER'S GUIDE TO MAKING AND MANAGING MONEY, 1996.

Accounting Methods

We haven't defined Income and Expense—(that is, when money is to be counted in these categories.) Here are the possibilities and they define the **Method of Accounting** you are using:

1. Cash Method: In this method you can include as income any money (cash or check) you have actually *received.* You can then include as expense any bills you actually *paid.* This method is commonly used by new businesses but can be very misleading as a management document. For example, when you get a $15,000 deposit, it will show as income whether or not you've actually earned it or even started the job. Or maybe you get behind on your bills and don't pay $32,000 of back bills. They don't show up as expense. Stop using this method as quickly as possible.

2. Billings Method (accrual): In this method you will count money as income if you've actually *billed* it—whether or not you've actually received it. You will count money you've been billed for as an expense whether or not you've actually paid it. A number of remodelers use this method but it is not the preferred method of accounting for remodelers because it can show misleading information on how much money has truly been earned and how much it has cost to earn that money.

3. Completed Contract Method: Here you won't record any income in your P & L until the job is *completed* and then you'll show all of it. You won't put any job cost expense in until the job is completed and then you'll put all the costs in. However, you'll show overhead expenses as they are paid. This method is often recommended for new construction but should not be used for remodeling. It produces reports that are extremely misleading. Your accountant may use this method, however for tax purposes.

4. Percentage of Completion Method: For each job that is in progress at the end of the month, you'll first revise the estimate to be sure it is accurate. Then you'll figure the percentage of those estimated costs that have been paid or are billed. That is the amount you will show as job cost expense on that job. By multiplying the anticipated contract amount by that same percentage you will arrive at the income earned on that job. Overhead is shown as billed or paid. *This is the method recommended for remodelers* who typically do jobs that extend more than a week or two in duration. Income shows the amount earned for the month and expense shows the amount it took to earn that income.

COACHING TIP

As soon as possible switch to *Percentage of Completion Method.* It's slightly more work but results in the most accurate management information to aid your decision making.

The Job Cost Report vs. the P & L

Each time you estimate a job, you are setting goals for what the project will cost to construct. While your P & L report shows how your job costs as a whole are coming in, the job cost report shows how each individual job is doing. Saying that a remodeler cannot be successful without timely and accurate job costs is no exaggeration for three reasons:

- Job costs give you the information you need to correct and update your estimating system.
- Job costs are your window on productivity and efficiency in the production department.

Job costs alert you that something is wrong and help you find out where. For most companies, job costs represent upwards of 60% of the overall company expenditures, and they cannot remain unexamined and unmonitored if you hope to control them and learn from them.

🐚 COACHING TIP

As consultants we work with many remodelers whose job costs are 5-15% off their estimate, robbing them of any net profit and often pushing the project into a loss. This is a very common cause of a lack of profitability in this business. Job cost reports let you stay on top of just how your estimating and your actual costs are matching up or diverging.

Three ingredients are needed to produce accurate job cost reports:

1. Prompt and fully filled out timecards clearly showing hours worked on each job.

2. Invoices from material suppliers with job names included and only one job's supplies listed per ticket.

3. Invoices from subcontractors by job name and only one job listed per ticket.

A job cost report is simply all the expenses of the job collected and matched against the estimated costs. This report can be done manually or with a computer. It's considerable work to produce manually but it has to be done. When your bookkeeping is computerized, job cost information is entered as you collect and pay bills and so producing job cost reports becomes very easy. Purchase software that includes completely integrated job costing so that entries need be made only one time. Not only is this easier but also helps minimize errors.

Job cost reports—especially those of jobs that have over-run—should be analyzed and discussed in a meeting with the salesperson, the lead carpenter, the production manager and the company owner. It's critical to stem erosion and find out how to avoid overruns in the future. If a job has overrun its budget but is still in construction, careful analysis may enable you to save money during the completion.

☞COACHING TIP

As you move deeper into the science of job costing, you will prob-ably want the actual labor hours broken down by task in the same grouping as you estimate (demolition, rough framing, setting doors and windows, etc.) Field people tend to hate this added work in filling out their timecards, your bookkeeper will spend considerable time logging it and you'll have to break down your estimate clear-ly into the same categories. It's well worth the effort—but only if the resulting data is consistently analyzed for patterns of overrun that can be corrected.

MANUAL JOB COST REPORT

This is an example of a very simple manually prepared job cost report with a minimum of categories tracked. As you can see, this remodeler has considerable work to do to bring estimates and actual costs into line.

	ESTIMATE	ACTUAL	VARIANCE
Labor	$ 720.00	$1,886.55	($1,166.55)
Plumbing	1,825.00	1,825.00	0.00
Millwork	0.00	345.68	(345.68)
Lumber	150.00	493.94	(343.94)
Electrical	290.00	260.00	30.00
Insulation	75.00	57.15	17.85
Drywall	530.00	488.35	41.65
Ceramic	1,260.00	1,200.00	60.00
Hardware	535.00	661.78	(126.78)
Misc.	150.00	258.25	(108.25)
	$ 5,535.00	$ 7,476.70	(1,941.70)

SAMPLE: COMPUTER GENERATED JOB COST REPORT

Job #95161   JOB BUDGET STATUS REPORT   by: J.J.
Simmons Job   DIRECT COSTS   08/28/95

Cost Category	Cost Category Descriptions	Budget	Paid to Date	Accrued Costs to Date	Budget Balance
110	Planning	200.00	84.00	84.00	116.00
200	Demo	0.00	87.74	88.00	(88.00)
210	Tear Out	260.00	140.00	140.00	120.00
520	Masonry	580.00	450.00	450.00	130.00
700	Wood Framing	2940.00	1344.55	1345.00	1,595.00
1200	Doors	853.00	112.54	113.00	740.00
1520	HVAC	240.00	350.00	350.00	(110.00)
1600	Electric	678.00	922.67	923.00	(245.00)
1700	Insulation	179.00	148.76	149.00	30.00
1800	Drywall	2127.00	2,096.26	2,097.00	32.00
2000	Millwork	436.00	1,201.53	1,201.00	(765.00)
2500	Clean Up	200.00	54.01	54.00	146.00
10000	Burden	0.00	864.42	864.00	(864.00)
		8,693.00	7,856.48	7,856.00	837.00

Linda W. Case, THE REMODELER'S GUIDE TO MAKING AND MANAGING MONEY, 1996.

Projecting Cash Flow

It can be very helpful to produce a simple cash flow report that tells you on Friday of one week, what your cash needs will be the next week. This is less important if you always have plenty of cash on hand. But most remodelers don't and this report projects any shortfall with at least a little notice so you can take action.

Some companies project cash flow over much longer periods which can be extremely valuable. If you feel you can do this accurately, it provides you with a great planning tool.

WEEKLY (MONTHLY) CASH FLOW PROJECTOR

Week (month) beginning _____

Beginning checkbook balance _____

INCOME:

SOURCE	AMOUNT	PICKUP DATE
_____	_____	_____
_____	_____	_____
_____	_____	_____

Total Income $_____

EXPENSES: (subs, suppliers, insurance, payroll and other)

PAYABLES WITH DISCOUNT

VENDOR	AMOUNT & DISCOUNT	DATE DUE
_____	_____	_____
_____	_____	_____
_____	_____	_____

Subtotal $_____

OTHER PAYABLES:

VENDOR	AMOUNT	DATE DUE
_____	_____	_____
_____	_____	_____
_____	_____	_____

Total Income $_____

Total Expenses $_____

Expected checkbook balance at end of week $_____
(Beginning checkbook balance+ income – expenses)

Linda W. Case, THE REMODELER'S GUIDE TO MAKING AND MANAGING MONEY, 1996.

The Balance Sheet

If the Profit and Loss Statement is the score of a ballgame, the Balance Sheet is the lifetime record of the team. Read properly, it contains the result of the current P & L and melds that into what the company owns and who has loaned the company money and more. While it is never as interesting as the current P & L to the entrepreneur, it is the most interesting and telling financial report to the bank, the bonding company or anyone who wants the full story on your company.

THE BALANCE SHEET SIMPLY PUT...

Assets = Liabilities + Owner's Equity

or

The value of what is owned = the value of the investment of others + your investment

---

The Three Balance Sheet Categories

Let's look at what the three main balance sheet categories represent and you'll see just how logical your balance sheet is. It's no harder to understand than that estimate for a porch enclosure!

ASSETS—What does the company have? This category includes anything of value whether it's paid for or not. Assets are listed in order of the speed with which you can convert them into cash.

Current assets are cash or can become cash or can offset the need for cash within 1 year.

Fixed assets are property of the company that usually will be owned for a long time like land, buildings, equipment. They are usually valued at the price paid and depreciation is shown on them (and subtracted from the price paid). Items under fixed assets are often difficult to assess for true value. For instance, goodwill may be carried here and what is that really worth? What is the office building really worth if we have to sell it quickly? These are difficult to judge.

LIABILITIES—Who do you owe for the assets? Another way to look at this is, other than you the owner, who owns the assets? the bank? your family? You may not have considered your lumberyard or your bank as "owning" part of your company but—in a sense—they do!

Current liabilities are obligations that must be paid within 12 months, like a short-term bank note, or accounts payable to your vendors and subcontractors. Payments owed within the next year on your vehicles would be listed here but those after 1 year would be long-term liabilities.

Long term liabilities are obligations which are not due for twelve months or more.

NET WORTH OR OWNER'S EQUITY—The value of the part of the company that you own. This is the excess of assets over liabilities. In a sense, you get the leftovers. What isn't owed to others is owned by you. In a partnership there would be an account for each partner. In a corporation, this would be Stockholders' Equity.

Under this section will be **Retained Earnings**, the total amount of net income retained over time for use by the business. If this is negative, then the business has been losing money (or conceivably has paid out more in dividends than it has earned).

Once you understand how a Balance Sheet is "built," it's easy to see why the value of what the company has must equal the value of what is owed to or owned by others. Now that we understand how to "read" the Balance Sheet, let's look at a sample Balance Sheet.

BALANCE SHEET

ASSETS
CURRENT ASSETS

Cash on hand	$ 100.00	
Checking	8,168.52	
Savings	70,134.31	
Accounts Receivable	41,461.59	
Employee Advances	200.00	
Due from Officer	47,567.53	
Prepaid Insurance	12,119.30	
*Costs in Excess of Billings	71,179.19	
Federal Estimated Taxes Paid	2,702.00	
State Estimated Taxes	2,000.00	
TOTAL CURRENT ASSETS		**$ 255,632.44**

PROPERTY, PLANT & EQUIPMENT

Equipment	$ 13,912.13	
Truck	24,474.04	
Less Accumulated Depreciation	(26,162.00)	
NET BOOK VALUE OF PROPERTY, PLANT & EQUIPMENT		**$ 12,224.17**

OTHER ASSETS

TOTAL OTHER ASSETS		**00.00**
TOTAL ASSETS		**$ 251,519.57**

LIABILITIES AND EQUITY
CURRENT LIABILITIES

Accounts Payable	$ 63,810.53	
* Billings in Excess of Costs	35,106.76	
FICA Taxes Payable	771.39	
Federal Taxes Payable	1,159.96	
State Taxes Payable	873.85	
City Tax Payable	341.67	
Note Payable	10,000.00	
Note Payable 1993 Vehicle	13,092.57	
TOTAL CURRENT LIABILITIES		**$125,156.73**

LONG-TERM DEBT

Loan from Shareholders	$ 00.00	
TOTAL LONG-TERM DEBT		**00.00**

STOCKHOLDERS' EQUITY

Common Stock	$ 500.00	
Paid in Capital	4,500.00	
Retained Earnings	140,002.56	
Profit and Loss	18,639.72	
TOTAL STOCKHOLDERS' EQUITY		**$126,362.84**

TOTAL LIABILITIES AND STOCKHOLDERS' EQUITY	**$251,519.57**

* Note: We know this Balance Sheet is based on percentage of completion because of these two entries.

Linda W. Case, *THE REMODELER'S GUIDE TO MAKING AND MANAGING MONEY, 1996.*

☞ COACHING TIP

Your job as financial manager is to be sure the company obtains the gross profit dollars it needs to pay overhead and net profit. Hopefully you've budgeted to see just what those dollars are for the year and the month. By looking at the gross profit still remaining in jobs in progress and the gross profit that is in the jobs you've sold but not yet begun, you can see how long the company could run on just that sum.

Let's take an example: let's say you need $20,000 a month in gross profit to cover overhead and net profit. As you review your jobs, you find there's $28,000 of unearned gross profit remaining in the jobs you are currently doing. Then there are two jobs waiting to start. The Mason job has $6,000 in gross profit in the sales price and the Hamers job has $7,500. Thus you have $28,000 +$6,000 + $7,500 = $41,500 or just over 2 months of gross profit sitting in backlog. Doing this calculation each month let's you establish a benchmark for your comfortable level of backlog. When you see your gross profit in backlog drop below the accustomed number you know you must get selling.

You may be tempted to hire new crews so you won't have any clients waiting for their job to start. Don't succumb to that temptation. Some level of backlog is helpful and necessary to all companies so that they can sell future work in a steady methodical manner rather than being forced to sell any job at any price quickly because a crew will be unemployed next Monday.

Who Will Produce These Reports?

The collection of financial data, for even a small remodeling company, is fairly vast. Many remodelers start out trying to do it themselves late in the evening after selling, estimating, and producing jobs. They tend to fall behind in keeping the books and the quality and timeliness of the information goes downhill from there.

Bookkeeping is organized financial record-keeping. Established procedures are used to track all job-related income and expenses. Unless you are unusually talented with numbers and have enough time to keep the books current, hire a trained bookkeeper. Here are some of your options:

1. An in-house bookkeeper/general office manager.

2 An outside freelance bookkeeper who balances the books monthly and provides the necessary reports for you to manage and to keep the government happy. This service is often available for under $300 a month.

3. A part-time bookkeeper who might work one day each week to do payroll and keep the books current.

☞ COACHING TIP

To further reduce your bookkeeping work, you can contract out the payroll function to a paycheck service. You call payroll in each week and checks are promptly issued. These services typically charge a minimum monthly amount based on a per-check fee, and they handle all tax reporting. It can be a real bargain for the small remodeler.

Consider paying personnel biweekly (every other week). You'll reduce the number of payrolls from 52 annually to 26 and save money. You may have to offer to "bridge" loans to personnel for the first few weeks so they can adjust to the two week pay period.

Finding an Accountant Who's a Team Player

Accounting analyzes, classifies, and accumulates the bookkeeping records into an historical picture that serves as a basis for future planning. It stores each financial transaction and provides reports for use in budget preparation as well as providing an audit trail for financial transactions.

Your accountant is likely to be an independent practitioner from whom you buy periodic (quarterly, semi-annually or annually) services. There are at least three roles your accountant should play for you:

➤ To prepare historical reports and filings in a timely manner and in a format easy for you to understand.

➤ To serve as a company advisor to help steer you toward profit and stability.

➤ To train you to become an effective financial manager.

Most accountants get good marks on the first task and poor marks on the other two. Be sure to make a firm agreement with your accountant that he or she will perform all three functions. Don't hesitate to change accountants if you feel you are getting second class service.

These first six chapters have focused on your role, your mission, empowering your personnel, setting financial goals and meeting them. This effort is summed up eloquently by a letter we received from Jim Strite, Strite Remodeling Company, Boise, ID, a remodeler who runs his business by the principles we've covered. He writes "This coming week my key staff and I will hold our semi-annual business meeting. We'll decide what to stop, continue, start for the last few months of the year. We're still on track for our projected volume but have dropped a point on gross profit. We'll implement strategies to pick up that drop. We'll review our goals for this year and compare projections to the actual. We'll make adjustments in writing and decide the person who will be accountable.

"Then our job is to return to the office and share the information with the full team. Everyone is working toward our goals, utilizing our mission statement because they have a stake in it! The 'stake' being a great place to work, lots of positive reinforcement, a learning organization and an above average wage with many benefits. Sounds easy. But as you already know it takes constant, disciplined, genuine, effective effort." Indeed it does.

7

Marketing for Pre-Sold Leads

Because marketing brings prospective customers to your door, it is an essential part of running a successful business. In fact, it's the fuel that powers your company machine.

Marketing = Every outreach from your company to your buying public that promotes your business, thereby attracting leads.

A successful marketing program will:

- Lessen the effects of the market's highs and lows by providing a steady flow of leads throughout the year.
- Produce quality leads that let you pick and choose the projects on which you want to work.
- Help you attract the types of customers with whom you enjoy working.
- Help you reposition your company so you're known in the community for new or expanded services.
- Pre-sell your company, making the sales process easier and less stressful.

◄── Position your company in such a way that your prospects will be willing to pay a professional fee for your services— helping you sell value, not price.

Many remodelers don't have a conscious marketing program. They take the passive approach and simply hope enough customers will materialize at their doors to keep them in business. They let the market dictate how much work they will do rather than aggressively tapping into their markets for the work they want. Savvy remodelers on the other hand, know that an aggressive marketing program is crucial to their success.

Market to Sell Value Not Price

When a remodeler begins in business, survival is usually foremost in their mind. Attracting business can be difficult when you don't have a track record. Often, young companies are forced to take numerous small jobs because they simply can't afford to be choosy. But as you grow, your goal is to have enough leads to allow you to "cherry pick" those jobs that you most enjoy and that produce the greatest profit. Marketing is your key to reaching that goal.

Only after you have "mined" all the referral leads you can from this ever-increasing group, should you begin marketing for cold prospects. If you are a small company, you may never need to go further than this Circle of Influence. This chapter will focus on how to market for quality referral leads. Chapter 8 will extend your marketing to prospects who don't know of your company but fit your prime customer profile.

Your first Marketing Goal is to create a loyal group of past customers and "friends of the company" who will refer others to buy from you and will themselves buy from you again and again. The referral leads generated from this Circle of Influence are significantly more likely to buy than a non-referred lead.

By reaching out to your community with marketing, your prospects will learn about the services and benefits that your company offers. When you walk in a prospect's home or office, they'll already know something about you and your company's expertise. Frequently, they have a good idea that you're not the cheapest company in town. This means that they've already accepted your professional level pricing because they realize that you deliver a superior product in a dependable manner—unlike your low priced competitors.

All successful and long-lived remodelers sell value and quality. *They do not sell price.* The communication of that value and quality is the role of your marketing program. Selling the lowest price is easy; it can hardly be called selling. Selling value and quality means real selling skills are needed as well as clear communication of these qualities in everything the company does.

Marketing for Referral Leads

Marketing includes a wide variety of activities such as establishing your company's market niche, developing your company image, creating a customer satisfaction program that prompts people to recommend your company to their friends and neighbors, public relations, and media advertising. The term marketing is a very broad one. In this chapter we'll focus on setting up your marketing program and then outreaching to your warmest potential leads. We'll cover these four critical marketing steps:

Step 1. Establishing a **Market Niche**

Step 2. Getting Your **Image** in Order

Step 3. Generating High Quality **Referral Leads**

Step 4. Developing a Powerful **Jobsite Marketing** Program

Step 1. Establishing a Market Niche

The most successful remodelers don't try to do all types of jobs for all types of people all over their geographic area. Rather, they carve out a particular segment of the broad remodeling market and concentrate their energies and resources on this specialty or *market niche*. They develop the products and services that allow them to serve that segment excellently. Then all of their marketing is targeted toward attracting customers within this niche.

Working in a niche is just deciding the who (the type of client), the what (the type of job), and the where (geographic area served) of the business. These elements must be meshed with your interest and the skills of your company and personnel.

Choosing a Profitable, Enjoyable Niche

A company niche can be defined by the:

- Type of **service** you offer—for example, this might be design/build or insurance reconstruction.

- Type of **property** you like to work on. Do you enjoy historic renovations or prefer retrofitting retail space?

- Type of **work** that your company does. Some remodeling companies specialize in creating additions on two-story colonials while others only handle interior work, such as kitchens and baths.

- **Geographic area** in which you prefer to work. While some remodelers will have customers throughout a metropolitan area, some only accept work in specific districts.

- **Products** you choose to use. Are you specializing in one kind of window? Or perhaps you've joined a franchise that represents one type of product.

ꙮ **Size** of your jobs. Do you like to do small jobs that can be completed in a week or less? Or would you rather stay with a job for more than a month?

ꙮ **Clientele** that you prefer to work with. Do you like to work with the wealthy? It's not for everyone. Some prefer the middle class market. Others market to seniors or the handicapped.

Factors for Choosing a Niche

Before committing to any niche, do some homework. Ask yourself these questions:

? Does the niche you have in mind have enough potential to support a profitable business? Is there enough opportunity in your immediate area? If not, how far will you have to travel to produce enough work?

? Will you enjoy the work you'll be doing? Money isn't everything. It's also important to like what you do.

? Are your employees trained in this type of work and can they do it well? If not, mistakes could happen which will quickly ruin your reputation.

? Does the work require specially trained workers? If so, is there a large enough base of employees to handle the work you plan on producing?

? Is the work profitable? What is the competitive atmosphere in the area?

? Will you be comfortable working with the clientele in this niche?

If you can answer all of these with a resounding "Yes!," then it's time to move forward.

EXAMPLES OF MARKET NICHES

- Kitchens and baths
- Room additions
- Large jobs designed by architects
- Roofing and siding
- Design/build
- Insurance reconstruction
- Decks, gazebos, screened porches
- Sunrooms and greenhouses
- Window replacement
- Handyman service
- Light commercial
- Historic restoration
- Medical and dental offices
- Retail space finishing
- Closet outfitting

VOICES OF EXPERIENCE...

Do Niches Work? In a landmark study of mid-sized firms called *The Winning Performance: How America's High Growth, Mid-Sized Companies Succeed,* Don Clifford and Dick Cavanaugh observed that 95% of the top performers in *every* sector of the economy were those with niche-creating, high-value-adding strategies.

John L. Stanton, Jr., Robert Linneman,
MAKING NICHE MARKETING WORK, McGraw-Hill, Inc., 1992

Step 2. Getting Your Image in Order

What image does the public have of your company? Your target market develops an image of your company from a variety of sources—your jobs, your signs, your personnel, your publicity, your brochures and other materials.

Image: the concept of a business or person that is held by the public.

Every good marketer works to control the quality of their image. It's crucial that all of the materials used to represent your company communicate a cohesive style that supports the niche you've chosen. A remodeler can claim that his or her company is professional, organized, and has design flair—but is that the way the public would describe it if asked?

Since remodeling is an easy-entry industry with plenty of companies coming and going each year, one of the first things you must do is communicate to the marketplace that your company is stable and will be around for a long time. Visually communicate that you're different—more professional, more reliable, more creative. You can do this with a creative array of company materials such as an attractive logo, stationery, sales and marketing tools, contracts and more.

Your company image includes every aspect of your company that is seen by the public—and that is considerable. Here are some key actions to consider:

- Remodeling Your Company Name
- Developing Your Company Logo
- Putting Your Image On Paper
- Developing a Company Brochure
- Maximizing Company Trucks: Your Traveling Billboards
- Using Your Office as Sales Tool

➤ Professionalizing Your Staff with Uniforms

➤ Signing to Send a Message

Remodeling Your Company Name

Many remodelers find themselves saddled with a name that doesn't communicate what they do in their business (Smith Associates) or which could mislead ("Smith Construction" when they are actually design build remodelers). This is a relatively easy problem to solve. "Smith" is the important part of this name and a change to "Smith Design and Remodeling" for instance, is a relatively small step. However, that change has some big benefits in marketing. Your signs and materials now clearly state what you do. Potential buyers are attracted just by seeing your company name—no explaining necessary.

Developing/Updating Your Company Logo

A logo is a graphic treatment of your company name. A logo may or may not include a graphic "symbol" as well. If you need a logo or if your logo needs to be updated, take the plunge and invest in the skills of a talented graphic designer to help you create a logo that has polish and flair. The investment for a corporate package design can range from $1,000 to $3,500 depending on the designer. Create a logo that you'll be happy with for the next 15-20 years and use it throughout all of your marketing efforts. Since you'll be working hard to establish this logo in the marketplace, you won't want to change in the near future.

BEFORE

CERTIFIED ROOFING SERVICES, Bladensburg, MD, updated their image with a new logo incorporating a contemporary typeface and a lively color combination of warm orange background and blue lettering.

AFTER

Putting Your Image on Paper

Now that your name and logo are developed, your designer or printer can convert them into a stationery package. Your package will include at least some of the following, depending on your budget and your needs:

- stationery
- second sheets
- note cards and envelopes
- fax sheets
- letter envelopes
- large envelopes
- labels
- rolodex cards
- business cards
- presentation folders
- business forms

If you have a stock of existing materials, transition into your new "look" piece by piece to avoid a huge outlay of cash at one time. Consider having your logo scanned into your computer so that you are able to add it to in-house forms.

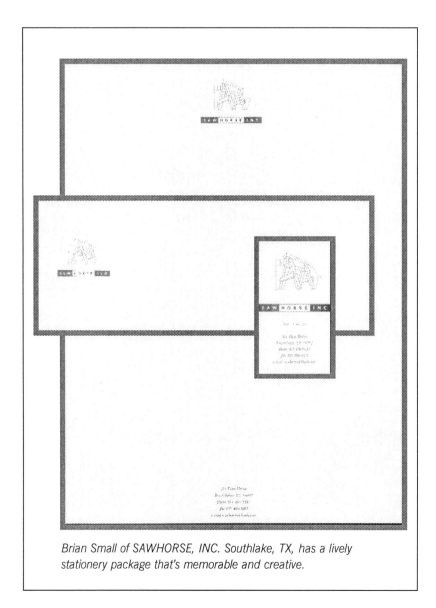

Brian Small of SAWHORSE, INC. Southlake, TX, has a lively stationery package that's memorable and creative.

Developing A Company Brochure

Often having a professionally designed brochure enhances your ability to sell jobs at a higher price. It's part of the packaging that goes along with professionalism. We're in the information generation. Prospects want something tangible left behind after your appointment. They want to take something away from your booth. Today's buyer wants information and they want to have it at their convenience.

It's hard to develop a brochure too early. Certainly by the time your company has grown to $500,000 in volume, a brochure will be helpful. Simple, one-color, brochures on stock paper can be developed for as little as 15 to 30 cents each.

Company Trucks: Your Traveling Billboards

If your company owns trucks that are well-kept and of recent vintage, use them as moving billboards with beautiful decals or painted signs. Many remodelers who have spent money this way say that it's one of their most effective lead generation tools. Stay away from the small, old-fashioned, magnetic signs that newcomers to the remodeling industry use. You're a pro, you charge more, and you must carry your creativity and class into every area of your business. Do it right or don't do it at all.

☞ COACHING TIP

The American Trucking Association and 3M Corporation studied the effectiveness of truck signs. They found that a delivery truck running 4 1/2 hours a day, 5 days a week in an urban area was seen by 5 million people a year. If you've already decided to have your own trucks, use them to make maximum marketing impact.

Matt Davitt of Davitt Design-Build, Inc., North Kingston, RI, offered his field personnel $1,000 toward the purchase of a new white truck if they would allow the company to decal it. His offer was enthusiastically received and he now has a fleet of moving billboards giving him high marketing impact at a minimal one-time cost. Be sure to check with your lawyer on the legal implications of adding your signage to the trucks of others.

YOUR REMODELING TEST

	S.J. JANIS Co.	COMPETITORS
OVER 45 YEARS IN THE REMODELING BUSINESS	✓	___
WISCONSIN NARI REMODELER'S AWARD FOR 7 CONSECUTIVE YEARS — 1989-1995	✓	___
MEMBER "BIG 50" REMODELERS HALL OF FAME	✓	___
CERTIFIED REMODELER ON STAFF	✓	___
COMBINED INDUSTRY EXPERIENCE OF OVER 100 YEARS	✓	___
COMBINED WORK HISTORY OF TRADE ASSOCIATES OF OVER 200 YEARS	✓	___
WISCONSIN CERTIFICATION—CONTRACTOR FINANCIAL RESPONSIBILITY: CERT. #2709	✓	___
CURRENT CERTIFICATES OF LIABILITY & WORKMENS COMPENSATION INSURANCE	✓	___
MEMBER OF NARI, METROPOLITAN BUILDERS ASSOCIATION, APA CODE PLUS • Program	✓	___
LIST OF CURRENT REFERENCES	✓	___
WRITTEN COMPANY WARRANTY	✓	___
ARCHITECTURAL DESIGNER ON STAFF	✓	___
DEGREED PROFESSIONALS ON STAFF	✓	___
FEATURED IN PUBLISHED ARTICLES IN TRADE MAGAZINES AND LOCAL NEWSPAPERS	✓	___
REGULAR PARTICIPANT ON WISN RADIO "MILWAUKEE'S REMODELING" PROGRAM	✓	___

This is your opportunity to test the remodeling companies you may be considering for work on your home.

Please take this opportunity to find out all you can about your prospective remodeling contractor.

The S.J. JANIS Company is an *experienced* Design/Build Remodeler—
We want to earn your trust and business!

S.J. Janis Company, Inc. • 3228 W. National Avenue • Milwaukee. WI 53215 • (414)384-4570

Gary Sannes, owner of S.J. JANIS COMPANY, INC., Milwaukee, WI, uses this clever "Remodeling Test" to tout his company's very special achievements. It's a way to get your prospect to learn about you and see that your competition just doesn't measure up.

Your Office as a Sales Tool

All remodelers have an office. Yours may be a room in the basement of your home, a large, well-decorated space in an office building, or a high-end showroom located in retail space. If it's open to consumers, it must project good workmanship, business success, and good organization. After all, prospective buyers are deciding whether to spend $10,000, $40,000, $100,000 or more with you, and those judgements are based on just such simple things as whether personnel seem friendly or whether the office looks organized and well designed. If your office is open to the consumer, be sure it sells for you.

Professionalize Your Staff With Uniforms

One of the easiest ways to differentiate your company from your competitor's is by incorporating uniforms for your staff. A company uniform can be as informal as a polo-style shirt imprinted with the company logo and worn with blue jeans—or as formal as matching shirt and pants with the name of the carpenter embroidered on the shirt. Your goal is to create name awareness for the company, while maintaining a consistently professional appearance for *everyone* who represents your company.

Company Signs Send A Message

Company signs are one of the most visible marketing tools you'll ever use. If your company is located in a building that allows signage, you have a powerful marketing tool at your disposal—don't waste it. Whether you're located on a busy retail street, or in an industrial park, your signage should be easily readable and consistent with the rest of your company materials. Your logo should be large enough to see and recognize. If your logo doesn't indicate your niche clearly enough, include a statement of your services such as *"The Best In High Quality Residential Remodeling."* Your telephone number should also be prominently listed. These rules stand for both building signage and job site signs.

Alan Derrick of DERRICK DESIGN AND REMODELING in Huntsville, AL has a distinctive logo and color combination (red, white, blue and black). His logo's angled-corner shape is echoed by his job signs and his brochure.

🔫 COACHING TIP

Remember, performing well is the very best image. Great looking trucks, beautiful stationery, a smashing office can never make up for doing poor work on the job. Underlying all your marketing must be your ability to do technically masterful work and do it quickly and neatly and with happy clients at the end.

Step 3: Generating High Quality Referral Leads

Remodeling magazine conducted a national survey of homeowners in 1991, and found that the first thing most people do when considering remodeling is to ask everyone they know "Do you know a good contractor?" The survey asked the homeowners to list the sources of referrals that they used to find a contractor. 70% counted on direct remodeling experience of their own or of their friends or relatives to help them find a contractor. Prospects prefer to work with someone who was referred to them. Take the time to create a system to capture these desirable referral leads.

Referrals are win-win. They give the homeowner assurance and trust in choosing a remodeler. For you, they deliver a prospect who values more than just price and is much more likely to buy than the random lead from the Yellow Pages or a newspaper ad. The close ratio on these leads far surpasses any other source of leads, plus it's one of the cheapest forms of leads. In addition, the referrer has given the prospect a great deal of information about your company that helps you make the sale.

Most referrals come from past customers and friends of the company, who represent a gold mine of leads. Unfortunately many remodelers look for gold everywhere but in their own back yard. But successful remodelers know a critical, proven principle of marketing:

The Golden Rule of Marketing: You will double the number of referral leads you receive if you constantly market back to previous customers and friends of the company.

Marketing for Referrals

Stay in touch with this special group of people through letters, personal telephone calls, gifts, a company newsletter, an invitation to an open house, a special note or message at

least 4 times per year. Some remodelers who know the importance of this referral base send information to their customers
up to 7 times each year! While the message is soft (no hard
selling here) your goal is to encourage referrals and capture
future business from this valuable group.

*Bruce Wentworth and Jerry Levine, WENTWORTH/LEVINE
ARCHITECT BUILDER, INC., Silver Spring, MD, produce this lively
newsletter for their past clients and interested prospects. It's
designed as a self-mailing trifold. Because they are a design/build
firm, every marketing outreach they make must be creative and
exhibit good design.*

Developing a Database

Much of your communication with your past customers and others will be through the mail. Create a database—a list of your past customers from at least the past five years—to which you have added others in your community who are likely to refer business to you. That list is best kept on computer—yours or someone else's. There are many software programs that make list management easy. If you want to subcontract the maintenance of your database, you'll find many resources in your community that can handle it for you. This allows you to easily order labels or addressed envelopes anytime you want to generate a mailing.

VOICES OF EXPERIENCE...

"Marketing enables you to hold on to your old customers. Many enterprises survive on repeat and referral business. Old customers are the key to both. When old customers don't hear from you or about you, they tend to forget you."

Jay Conrad Levinson, GUERRILLA MARKETING, Houghton Mifflin, 1984.

Saying Thanks With Customer Gifts

In order to send you referrals, your clients must feel good about your company. Many remodelers keep their customers feeling good about their company by presenting them with a token of their appreciation at the end of the project. A gift lets your customers know that you value the business they've given to your company.

🎺 COACHING TIP

Be sure to say *Thanks* for every referral. Write a note or phone to thank the person who sent the lead your way. Some remodelers enclose a gift certificate (perhaps a $10 certificate to the local bookstore you remodeled—make both clients happy—or a certificate to a gourmet bakery) or a lottery ticket (thanks a million!) as a special thanks. Every business has people who refer and refer and refer. They're very special supporters of your company. Say thanks by taking them to lunch or to the ballpark or to the theater. They need to know that you value their support.

Employee Referrals

Referrals by employees are equally as valuable as referrals from former customers. If your employees are happy, loyal and enthusiastic about your company and the kind of work you do, they will bring back referrals too. Encourage them by providing them with business cards to hand out to friends and associates. Have contests for the employee who brings in the most referrals. Create a bonus program to reward their loyalty.

Business Contacts Deliver Business

While referrals from clients are wonderful, don't overlook those that can result from your business relationships. Create a referral program for your business allies to encourage them to bring business your way. The most effective method of encouraging referral leads from your business associates is by maintaining a healthy personal relationship with all of your contacts. Make it a policy to take a contact out to lunch at least once per month. Keep those relationships alive and thriving.

While all types of businesspeople can be strong referrers, here are some specialties that remodelers particularly rely on:

- Real estate agents
- Insurance adjusters
- Subcontractors
- Suppliers
- Architects
- Bankers
- Landscape companies
- Builders
- Specialty remodelers

Step 4: Developing a Powerful Jobsite Marketing Program

The ability to use your jobsites to market your services provides you with a tremendous advantage. A jobsite provides a valuable marketing outpost for selling your remodeling services to neighbors who often share the same worn-out roof, inefficient windows, outdated kitchen or bath, or outmoded floor plan as the house you're remodeling.

Grab Their Attention with Great-Looking Job Signs

A great-looking job site sign in the yard of a customer tells the neighborhood that your company has been hired by people just like them. Site marketing produces referral quality leads since the prospect can approach the people in their neighborhood that have used your services. And site signs are a proven, effective marketing tactic that produces quality leads at a very low price. A New England remodeler revamped his signage to be oversized, bright, and well-designed and saw leads jump 20% as a result. If your signs aren't pulling in leads now, they may need help!

To be effective, site signs should be simple and easy to read from a distance. They should contain the company name and phone number, logo, and slogan. If the company name does not suggest remodeling to the reader, the sign can say "Another High-Quality Remodeling by..." or something similar. Look around. Today's site signs are also highly creative. They may be lighted or landscaped. They may be created from wood or wrought iron. But the one common element is that the best signs all exhibit wonderful craftsmanship.

Neighborhood Marketing

The people who own the homes surrounding your current jobs are excellent prospects. Don't miss this opportunity to attract business from these homeowners. A well thought-out program will help establish your company name in the neighborhood and encourage these prospects to keep an eye on your progress. For many remodelers, this is a mainstay of their lead generation program.

When a job is underway in a neighborhood, take advantage of the opportunities to approach neighbors by mail or by dropping off literature in person. Many remodelers target 25 to 50 neighboring houses for this kind of campaign.

🏀 COACHING TIP

Your job site is like a factory showroom right there in the neighborhood. By drawing attention to the job site with signs, mailings, and other tactics, you'll have the opportunity to show off your company's skills both in construction and in the demeanor of your staff. Don't forget to talk to your subcontractors about the importance of professionalism as well. Because you'll have the entire neighborhood watching, keeping your job site clean and neat is a must!

Hanging Your Message: Using Door Knob Hangers

Door knob hangers are marketing pieces meant to be left hanging on the door knob of homes in the area immediately surrounding a job. They can be used as part of a canvassing program or as a free-standing means of generating telephone calls to your office. While studies show that homeowners don't like materials attached to their houses, many remodelers attest to their value as lead-getters.

Let Your Feet Do The Walking: Effective Canvassing

Simply put, canvassing is selling door-to-door. The goal is to talk to a homeowner face-to-face with the objective of setting an appointment for a full presentation by a company salesperson sometime in the next few days.

It's a marketing technique that's been around forever and some companies find it a very effective addition to their overall marketing program. When canvassing is done on a small scale with the production manager or company owner talking with homeowners around a job site, it is fairly easy. However, when done on a large scale with professional canvassers, it is a difficult form of marketing requiring canvassers that can handle constant rejection. It's a technique most suited to the middle class market—and to specialty products. But make no mistake about it, canvassing sells.

Show Off With An Open House

A project open house can be a wonderful way to show off your company's workmanship and generate very high quality leads from the neighborhood. Remodelers around the country have benefitted from allowing prospects and customers to walk through a completed project, touching, feeling and seeing the spectacular results they've created.

Before you begin, you'll need three vital ingredients to make it work—a noteworthy project, welcoming clients and a seasonable time of year. You'll be surprised at how many clients are willing, even honored, to open their homes. Plants or an item you know they need, such as a microwave, make thoughtful thank you gifts. Most neighbors have a hard time passing up the opportunity to see another's home. If they aren't ready to remodel today, they'll be ready within the next five years!

Marketing for Pre-Sold Leads

This chapter has focused on getting the best leads—referral leads—for relatively little expenditure. No company can bypass this high value, relatively inexpensive aspect of marketing. Chapter 8 focuses on tactics to use when you need more leads than can be generated from past clients, friends of the company, and your jobsites. Then Chapter 9 provides budget guidelines and tips on how and why to measure and monitor your marketing.

Remember, marketing is your best tool for generating consistent, high quality business.

8

Marketing to New Prospects

You've created an excellent marketing program for the past customers and friends of your company. That program attracts top quality leads—but perhaps not enough for your needs. Now you need to reach beyond your Circle of Influence to prospects who may not be aware your company exists. How do you do this most cost efficiently?

Your primary marketing goal is reaching those people who are most likely to become your company's customers. The marketing tactics you use must entice these prospects to come to your company for their remodeling needs.

A good rule of marketing is to look for new buyers who fit the same socioeconomic (financial), geographic, and psychographic (lifestyle) profile as those who buy from you now. They comprise your prospects. So in order to focus on your company's best prospects, you must first know what market you're targeting. Then determine the best ways to reach this profitable audience.

Your outreach to new prospects could take many directions:

- Direct Mail
- Telemarketing

- Media Advertising
- Radio
- Television
- Home and Mall Shows
- Publicity
- Networking
- Teaching a Course
- Charitable Event
- Remodeled Home Tour

Each tactic has its pros and cons. Experiment each year and find those lead generation methods that work best for your company, generating high quality leads at a reasonable cost. We'll cover budgeting in the next chapter.

Target Prospects With Direct Mail

Direct mail advertising is the mailing of promotional literature to a list of prospective buyers in groups of 25 to 50,000 or more. Direct mail is a fairly common type of marketing but can be very expensive. Its success or failure depends on the quality of the mailing list and also upon the quality of the mailed material. Here are guidelines to make your direct mail campaign a success:

1. The first hurdle is getting the consumer simply to open the envelope. Think of how you handle your direct mail (sometimes known as "junk" mail). Each day you get a pile of mail, sort through it quickly and then toss, unopened, the material you know you don't want. Your company's direct mail must somehow bypass the trash can! For this reason many remodelers have found success with postcards.

713 469-6057

*Voted One of America's Top 50 Remodeling Companies**
*Remodeling Magazine

We provide:

INTEGRITY: We keep our word and our reputation proves it.

DETAILED PROPOSALS: Easy to read computer generated proposals detail your plans and project cost.

SUPERIOR COMMUNICATION: Pre-construction conferences, daily progress reports and written change orders keep us in sync every step of the way.

JOB SITE ETIQUETTE: Prompt arrival, clean unifor employees, courteous manners and daily demonstrate our professional attitude to your project.

We are:

QUALIFIED: National Certified Graduate Remode

FULLY INSURED: Customer, Employees and Subc

Call for your project consultation and a co
713 469-6057

Don Strong and
Michael Strong, CGR, of
BROTHERS STRONG, INC.
in Houston, TX, developed
this postcard to emphasize
their strong credentials.
They have packed
the back of the card
with lots of valuable
information in an
easy-to-read format.

2. Success in direct mail equals a 1 to 2 percent response rate. Some direct mail experts believe that mailing three times to the same recipient is better than mailing to three different lists. One Kansas City remodeling firm successfully targeted 4,200 prime buyers in their market and directed a different (and intriguing) mailing piece to these recipients each month. Their sales response was excellent.

3. Include a call-to-action in every direct mail piece you create. Urge the prospect to respond immediately by mentioning a limited time, a special offer (a free microwave oven with every kitchen installed by September 25), or free information (100 Ways To Double Your Storage Space).

In your call-to-action, decide what you want them to do and tell them how to do it. Do you want them to call for an appointment? Visit your showroom? Call for additional information?

4. Readers are more likely to respond if you reduce their risk of doing so. Write about a no-obligation appointment, or "no salesperson will call," or "satisfaction guaranteed." Make it easy for them to take action by displaying a toll-free number prominently, enclosing a self-addressed envelope or attaching a postage-paid Business Reply Card.

5. Measuring the response is vitally important with high risk, high cost methods like direct mail. Each mailing should be individually analyzed to determine the mailing list used, the piece sent, the number of leads generated, and the number of sales closed. Constant monitoring is the only way to educate yourself about what really works for you in direct mail.

Telemarketing Increases Marketing Impact

Telemarketing is the selling of goods and services by telephone. For the remodeler, the goal is to generate interest from the prospect, then set an appointment for a presentation by a company salesperson within the next few days.

While a minority of remodelers (particularly specialty companies) are now using telemarketing, it's becoming more popular as an effective addition to a successful marketing program. Telemarketing is unique among marketing methods in that the phoner is in direct contact with the potential buyer and is able to respond, meet objections, and close. If it's to be effective, the message must be carefully chosen and made uniform. It is also the marketing method that enrages a large segment of the homeowner population when their dinner or bath is interrupted by an unwelcome call.

While telemarketing can cost as much as four to six times more than direct mail, it's only one-tenth the cost of a person-to-person sales call. And it can produce response rates five to ten times higher. This marketing tactic can be used by almost any remodeler—on either a large or small scale. The effort can be as simple as an employee calling the owners of the 20 homes surrounding each project or as complex as a multi-person "boiler room" operation with phoners making hundreds of calls per day.

Media Advertising

Media advertising can reach a large number of people—however many of them may not be candidates for your products or services. This can be a huge waste of your marketing dollars —but if done right, can also deliver dozens of high quality leads. Because you're reaching such a large audience, these tactics tend to be expensive and produce lower quality leads than those tactics covered in Chapter 7.

For companies with small marketing budgets, these marketing tactics should be used *only* after you have implemented the other more effective methods of marketing discussed previously. However, companies requiring a huge number of leads to reach their sales volume goals may need media advertising.

Media advertising includes all print ads (newspapers, magazines, billboards) or broadcast commercials (network or cable television, radio).

Composing an Ad

The three most important principles of putting an ad or a commercial together are:

◄ Target a specific audience—the contractor's prime customer. You can do this in two ways—by the media you choose and by the message you send.

◄ Stress benefits to the reader or listener because they are always asking "What's in it for me?"

◄ Give the reader or listener a reason to take action now rather than later.

Most remodelers turn to a professional for ad or commercial preparation. But the professional brings only half the needed information to the table. The professional may know advertising, but he/she needs input on the remodeling business, the targeted remodeling buyer, and the type of work you want. Often you can find and use a relatively inexpensive graphic artist who can take your ideas and turn them into an artistic and effective ad.

Advertising Opportunities in the YELLOW PAGES

The *Yellow Pages* are unique among advertising resources in that they are used by a consumer who is already intending to buy. Surveys show the consumer is persuaded to call a contractor first by previous awareness of the business and then by the size of the ad. Any remodeler is well served by at least a small listing in the *Yellow Pages*. Such a listing will "catch" those consumers who (a) might remember the remodeler when they see the name or (b) who are using the *Yellow Pages* to find your company's number.

If consumers don't recognize a company, the size of the ad then becomes important. However, the size of your ad should be relative to the sizes of your competitors' ads. If the largest ad in your category is a 1/8 page, there's no need for you to buy a full page in order to stand out. A slightly larger 1/4 page would be more than sufficient. Therefore, study the size of the ads already appearing under "Home Improvement" or the category listing you want to enter before deciding what size display ad to buy.

Yellow Pages ads should list your areas of specialty, your association affiliations, license number, years in business (if it is reasonably long), and note whether financing is available.

☞ COACHING TIP

The effectiveness of YELLOW PAGES advertising seems to be quite different depending on whether your company is full line or specialty. Full line companies find YELLOW PAGES ads very weak yet expensive. However, many specialty remodelers are happy with the response they receive from their ads.

Newspaper Advertising

Newspapers reach hundreds of thousands of readers each day and can be a wonderful spot in which to place your message. Because newspapers are printed daily or weekly, their material is very timely, allowing you to quickly reach their audience with specials, sales, or announcements. Your message can reach a very large audience for only a few pennies per person. In addition to the large, metropolitan newspaper in your city, dozens of smaller newspapers target selected markets and can be a much better purchase for your company. However, because not all readers of a newspaper are your prospects, you could be wasting money too.

Here are some tips for creating print advertising that works:

- Consistency, frequency and patience are the keys to a successful campaign. Plan to run your ad many times before you can expect to generate results. Unless you're running a special offer, such as a sale, several exposures to your message will be required before most people will act.

- Include a strong "call-to-action" in your ad. Tell your prospects what you'd like them to do after reading your ad —visit your showroom, call for a free estimate or design consultation, or call for a free informational brochure.

- Ads with photos generate more responses than ads without photos or ads with illustrations. But because the reproduction quality of newspapers is quite low, the quality of any black and white photos you use must be high.

- Only create one or two ads for your entire campaign. Studies show that a single ad can be used effectively for up to nine months without a reduction in response.

This simple black and white newspaper insert by John Sylvestre, **SYLVESTRE CONSTRUCTION, INC.**, Minneapolis, MN, makes clear that the company both designs and constructs. It can also be used for jobsite mailings or general prospect mailings.

Magazines

Magazines are another way to reach a broad market base. However, there are pro's and con's in magazine advertising.

Pro's:

○ Magazines are beautiful and, because of the quality of the publication, photography can really shine.

○ Magazine subscribers tend to be very loyal readers and pick up a magazine several times over the course of a month.

○ Magazines have a long shelf-life—they're not thrown away for at least a few weeks.

Con's:

◐ Because magazines come out only once a month, it's difficult to promote sales or other specials that run for a short time. Therefore, companies tend to use "institutional" ads that can be good for creating an image for the company over the long term, but less effective in generating solid leads immediately.

◐ Magazine lead time is long. Your ad must be delivered up to six weeks before it will appear. This means that you're stuck if your needs change.

◐ The costs of magazine advertising can be prohibitive.

COACHING TIP

We generally try to discourage our clients from using magazine advertising because of the cost versus the uncertainty of the result. Advertise here only if you have all your other bases covered and want to experiment.

Radio

Radio is a relatively inexpensive ad medium. Ninety-nine percent of American homes have radios and approximately 50 million new radios are sold each year. But the advertiser has only sound to work with—so the message is fleeting. Prime time is the morning and evening drive time, when audiences are the largest and advertising is the most expensive. Commercials are sold in 10, 30, and 60 second spots and are packaged with placement time and frequency.

Radio listeners are loyal to a particular station, and station content is carefully targeted to a particular demographic audience. Many stations focus on very narrow bands of listeners, such as a specific ethnic group, business professionals, teens or older listeners. When you're choosing a radio station, pick the one with demographics closest to your prime customer. This probably means homeowners in the 30-65 years of age category.

COACHING TIP

A number of remodelers are on the radio with weekly call-in home improvement shows. They neither pay nor are paid but get excellent exposure in their marketplace. Would this work in your market?

Television

Advertising on television is the form of advertising that is most like personal selling. You're in the consumer's home and they can see and hear your ad. With good television advertising, your local company can soon seem like a nationally recognized name. Because of its cost, television advertising has commonly been used by only the largest remodeling companies. But now, with the abundance of cable television stations available at attractive rates, television is becoming more popular for companies of all sizes.

Television commercials must be professionally produced— either by the station or an ad agency and you'll usually be charged for the production. For the larger remodeler, television can be a powerful supplement to the marketing plan.

Home & Mall Shows

Home and mall shows can be outstanding opportunities to meet and talk to hundreds or even thousands of potential buyers. Home and mall shows are not the same. The home show visitor has paid money to spend some time looking and thinking about purchases related to the home. They're focused on the same theme as the exhibitors.

Mall show visitors have happened upon the show while they've been visiting the mall for other purposes. Because they're not as focused, mall show leads are generally of lesser quality than home show leads.

Before committing to any show as a part of your marketing mix, do your research. If possible, visit the show before you decide to sign up. Check the traffic pattern. Interview exhibitors. That way you can scope out how successful the show is and how it will do for you.

Staffing will be one of the most costly aspects of participating in shows. To get the most out of a show, your booth must be manned at all times. This can mean 10:00 am to 10:00 pm in some cases. These long days will require two or more shifts of knowledgeable employees.

Booth space is usually sold in units of square feet—10' x 10' is a common booth size. The size increases in 10' increments— 10' x 20', 10' x 30', etc. Whatever space you choose, design your booth to be open, comfortable and beautifully furnished.

Company Display Materials must be professional and very eye-catching. Many companies develop ingenious, reusable booths, which cuts their costs over time. Read the rules of the show to see whether you will be allowed to set up the booth or will need to hire expensive union show workers to do so.

Give-aways can range from company brochures or special promotion flyers to specialty items like yardsticks and magnets complete with the company name. Be sure the prospects walk away with some materials including the company name, address and telephone number.

Take the time to qualify the prospects that come through your booth. Some remodelers accept every person who walks in the booth as a lead. Then they don't have the time or staff to follow up on all of them. If you can't follow up, the money you have invested has been wasted. So it's much more effective to be very selective in who you designate as a "lead."

The brochure developed by **LEE KIMBALL KITCHENS**, Boston, MA, is simple but elegant in design. The graphics including the treatment of the steps make it seem friendly and easy-to-read.

Generating Publicity: Spotlight Your Company

Publicity is the art of getting your name or that of your company in the media. It's one of the most valuable forms of marketing, providing a highly credible third-party testimonial to the quality of your company. And, it's easier than you think.

The first step to generating publicity is to create a **database** of media contacts at newspapers (especially the smaller, local publications), industry publications, magazines, and association publications. You can find this information at your local library. Everyone in your media database should receive **at least 4-6 press releases** about you and/or your company each year.

The second step is to think of **newsworthy topics** that your press releases might address. Be creative. Many activities that you think are mundane actually have news value. Here are some ideas for press releases. Have you:

- attended a national convention (Headline idea: *Local Remodeler Attends National Industry Convention.*)
- taught a class on remodeling
- been featured in a national magazine (*Local Remodeler Featured in National Publication*)
- earned an industry designation
- won an award
- attended an educational seminar
- written an article for a trade publication
- donated time or materials to a local charity
- had an office open house
- celebrated a company anniversary
- begun to carry a new product
- hired a new employee

Don't be discouraged if the large, metropolitan daily newspapers don't pick up your releases. They're besieged with press releases from hundreds of companies. Instead, concentrate on the smaller publications that always look for filler articles.

Once an article is written about your company, cut it out and send **reprints** to your customer base. Include a copy of the article in your presentation book. Remember, people believe what they read. And this third party testimonial is powerful for your company image.

Sample Press Release

FOR IMMEDIATE RELEASE   Contact: Elizabeth Peters
                         Wk. (301) 588-8172
                         Hm. (301) 000-0000

Local Remodeler Wins National Award

June 7, 1998—Silver Spring, MD—Bob Smith, president of All American Remodeling, was awarded the Superior Gold Award for Excellence in Workmanship from the National Association of Remodelers, USA. NARU President, Rebecca Oliver said, "All American Remodeling is the epitome of professionalism in remodeling today. Their concern for the quality of their product, as well as their excellence in customer service, makes this company one of the best."

Bob Smith has successfully operated All American Remodeling, a full service remodeling company located in Silver Spring, MD, since 1980. "I'm truly honored to be the recipient of this award," said Smith, "I'm delighted that our efforts to constantly improve have been noticed by our peers."

Smith, one of the state's few Certified Reliable Remodelers (CRR), has won several awards in the past for both personal and professional achievement.

###

Networking: Person-To-Person Lead Generation

Networking is simply a matter of building relationships with people who can help your business either by bringing direct sales or by sending referral leads. While it might seem that meeting and talking with people is a natural activity that doesn't need a system, experts agree you can maximize your impact with strategy. Here are some tips on how to begin:

○ Create a high profile for your company within the community. Join a local organization—it might be the local Chamber of Commerce, the Rotary Club or the Elks—and then participate. Show up for meetings and volunteer for a committee.

○ Take a business associate—supplier, someone from your industry association, another business acquaintance—to breakfast or lunch once a month.

○ Suppliers are a steady source of referrals. Take them out to lunch and ask for their advice on how to make your company stronger. They'll be flattered and you'll receive some wonderful input—and future leads.

Teach an Adult Education Course

Remodelers across the country are coming in contact with quality prospects while they're teaching adult education courses sponsored by their community college or other local organization. Some programs are technical—like framing or masonry. Others are more general—*How to Plan Your New Kitchen* or *Working with a Design/Build Remodeler.*

Homeowners who attend these classes are excellent prospects. Many times consumers don't understand the complexity inherent in a remodeling project and when they find out—they hire a professional to handle it! You'll be in the catbird seat. Of course, you have to be organized and knowledgeable about the subject you'll be teaching.

PROJECT
THE CLASSIC
SCREEN PORCH

CUSTOMER
JEFF & LISA
CLARK

PROJECT
MANAGER
MARK CHRISTENBERRY

DESIGNER
BOB FLEMING

True Southern Charm! The screen bays on this porch are as wide as possible with traditional style railings which replicate that look of an old southern porch. The views are maximized, the bugs are eliminated, and the screening tends to disappear. The gable roof, with a high vaulted ceiling inside, allows the maximum amount of natural light to reach the existing interior room just behind the new porch. The ceiling is nicely finished with traditional beaded ceiling boards. Finally, the owner has selected just the right colors to accent the porch furnishings.

CLASSIC
REMODELING
& CONSTRUCTION, INC.

763-3297

Bob Fleming, CLASSIC REMODELING & CONSTRUCTION, INC., Charleston, SC, has developed a number of project sheets over the years. Once designed, they are color copied in small quantities for inclusion with proposals or to give prospects information on jobs similiar to the project they are contemplating.

Participate in Charitable Events

You can reach some excellent prospects by participating in charitable events around your community. For many remodelers this is just an extension of community efforts in which they are already involved. Other remodelers decide to sponsor or participate in Habitat for Humanity or Christmas in April so they can do good for others while doing well for themselves.

If your target market is the highly affluent, you may choose to donate time or materials or cash to organizations that are favorites of the well-to-do. This will show your preferred audience that you're not just a "taker" but are willing to give back to the community that supports your company. Schools and clubs often use auctions as fundraisers. Consider donating "A Carpenter For A Day" to the auction.

Join a Remodeled Home Tour

From time to time, an organization in your community will sponsor a Remodeled Home Tour—a selection of remodeled homes that interested people can tour for a small fee. Depending on the organization, this can be an effective way to show off your work to dozens of prospects. If you have the chance to participate, make sure you market the event. Don't rely just on the marketing of the sponsoring organization.

Reaching Out to the Universe of Prospects

In this chapter we've focused on getting our message out to completely new prospects—people who know nothing about our company and must be reached by advertising or personal contact with us or our work. Now let's talk budgets and measuring results.

9

░░

Budgeting, Managing, and Monitoring Your Marketing

Marketing is an investment in your future. It means spending money in anticipation of your return. You want to spend that money wisely and and feel assured that it is working well for you.

How Much Should You Spend on Marketing?

We've all heard the saying, "It takes money to make money." Well, in marketing, it takes money to generate leads. By spending your dollars on marketing, you're investing in the future of your business. You're betting that you'll be able to create a consistent flow of quality leads that will translate into more profits and more success for your company by spending those lead generation dollars.

Typical marketing budgets for full-line remodeling companies are in the range of 2—5% of the *projected* yearly volume. What you'll need to spend depends on your average job size. If job sizes are small, you'll probably need the full 5%. If your company works in the rarefied niche of very large projects (over $75,000) a 1-2% budget will be enough to put together a very effective program.

Specialty or single line remodeling companies should budget between 10%–15% of projected volume. Specialty companies must spend more money because they need a much higher *quantity* of leads than most full-line companies since individual job sizes are smaller.

Your marketing budget should include:

- design of company materials
- printing
- postage
- photography
- uniforms
- job site signs
- brochures
- media costs
- and anything else that is created to help your company generate leads.

While this amount of money can sound high, remember that *it also includes the cost of the personnel to implement the program.*

VOICES OF EXPERIENCE...

When considering how to spend your marketing dollars, keep in mind the advice of Jay Conrad Levinson, author of *Guerrilla Marketing* (Houghton Mifflin, 1984):

○ **Spend 10%** of your marketing investment on everyone in your market area. This could be done with newspaper or radio advertising, for example.

- **Spend 30%** of your marketing investment on your prospects. Prospects could be the neighbors surrounding job sites, homeowners in a particular neighborhood, or people with homes of a certain age.

- **Spend 60%** of your marketing investment on previous customers and friends of the company.

Use Co-op Advertising Funds

You may find that your suppliers would like to help you market so you can sell more jobs and use more product. Remodelers often neglect the availability of co-op advertising funds. Co-op funds are made available by manufacturers and/or distributors of products that you use. Your co-op allocation often depends on the amount of materials you've purchased in a year. Some companies don't set limits on funds but ask to approve the marketing tactic before they'll give you the money. Co-op funds often can be used for in-house marketing pieces like brochures as well as newspaper, magazine and radio advertising.

To receive co-op funds, you'll be asked to include a manufacturer or distributor logo or slogan on any marketing you fund with these dollars. Often the logo can be small and unobtrusive, giving you a marketing piece at half the normal cost.

All contributions to your marketing budget are welcome so be sure to research co-op availability.

Monitoring Your Leads and Sales

Monitoring the results of your lead generation programs help you make sure that you're using your money and time to attract highly targeted leads for just the kind of work you want—fun and profitable! This monitoring is more than counting the **quantity** of leads. It is reviewing their cost and—most importantly—checking their **conversion rate** into sales. To fully monitor your leads check the **average sales price** of the sales created by a certain tactic. For instance, *Yellow Pages* leads might generate sales averaging $11,080, while your home show might deliver leads producing sales averaging $15,837. That's an important difference in quality that will affect how you allocate your marketing money next year.

When you can assess the effectiveness of any marketing tactic on the following four measures, you are taking charge of your marketing. You will make informed decisions on which lead generation tactics work and which don't based on:

- quantity of leads generated
- cost per lead
- conversion rate (close rate) into sales
- average size of sale.

Use a simple Lead and Sales Tracking form to gather information manually, or buy computer lead tracking software.

Lead and Sales Tracking Form

SOURCE	# OF LEADS	EXPENSE	$/LEAD	# OF SALES	$/SALE	% CONVERSIONS	AVG. JOB $
Referrals							
Job Site Signs							
Vehicle Signs							
Canvassing							
Direct Mail to Jobsites							
Yellow Pages							
Publicity							
Newspaper Ads							
Magazine Ads							
Radio							
Television							
Home Shows							
Mall Shows							
Telemarketing							
Canvassing							
Direct Mail							
Other:							
TOTAL							

Here's a sample entry:

SOURCE	# OF LEADS	EXPENSE	$/LEAD	# OF SALES	$/SALE	% CONVERSIONS	AVG. JOB $
Newspaper Ads	45	$1800.00	$40.00	15	$120	33%	$21,640

*Linda Case and Victoria Downing, THE REMODELER'S MARKETING POWERPAK,
Remodeling Consulting Services, Inc., 1995.*

Establishing Close Ratio

The *close ratio* is your company's relationship between the number of leads that have come in and the number of jobs sold. Like all statistics, it has to be examined over time. Generally full-line remodelers look for a close ratio of 1 sale out of 4 or 5 qualified leads. Thus, 20 to 25 percent of their sales calls produce a sale which provides a healthy level of sales activity. You want to track the number of lead calls into your office, the number of first sales calls and the number of sales.

Specialty firms, depending on their lead-gathering strategy, may make more sales calls to sell one job. Some small, referral-based remodelers may sell 30 to 40 percent or more of their sales calls. This high percentage is often a sign that they could market more, raise their markup, and probably increase their volume if they desire. However, then they would see a drop in the close ratio to more normal levels.

A poor close ratio means poorly targeted marketing or inadequate sales ability or both. If your company has two or more salespeople, you want to compare close ratios between them. Sometimes owners feel there is no loss in having a salesperson who doesn't sell well if they're paid on commission, since they only get paid for the jobs they do sell. However, that salesperson is wasting valuable leads. No company can afford a non-performing salesperson.

Establishing a company close ratio can also help in projecting the number of leads needed to provide a certain targeted volume. For example, if you want to sell $500,000 in a year and know that your average job size is $10,000 (50 jobs) and that the sales staff closes 1 out of 4 leads, you knows that the firm will need 200 leads to produce that volume. Those leads can then be tracked on a monthly basis to be sure the firm is on target.

Leads are gold to the remodeler and must be handled as such. They require careful analysis so that precious sales time and effort is not wasted. Only with an effective lead-handling program can the remodeler be sure that sales talent, time, and money are being spent in the most effective way.

Developing Your Marketing Plan

Impulsive investing in individual marketing tactics is the poorest, most inefficient way to spend your marketing dollars. Instead create a balanced marketing plan on paper and spread the tactics through every month of the year.

Sample Marketing Program

$500,000 Remodeler
Marketing Budget 3% = $15,000
Average Job Size = $15,000
Needs 33 jobs/year
Closes 1 out of 4 qualified leads
Needs 132 qualified leads for the year
Needs 11 leads a month.

Company Image Materials

Update logo	$ 1000.00
Develop brochure	1200.00
Paint one truck	650.00
Business Cards for lead carpenters	75.00
Uniforms	300.00
SUB-TOTAL	$3225.00

Circle of Influence Program

60 Thank You Notes	$ 50.00
Customer Gifts	300.00
Four Mailings	465.00
SUB-TOTAL	$ 815.00

Prospect Program

Job Site Mailings	$ 530.00
Freelance assistance	1000.00
Job Sign Upgrade including labor for building	250.00
Two open houses	1600.00
Float in 4th of July Parade	400.00
Networking through professional memberships. Dues and regular meetings	660.00
Yellow Pages Listing	360.00
Ad in Softball League Directory	250.00
SUB-TOTAL	$ 5050.00
10% contingency fund	$ 1500.00
Staff to implement plan	4160.00
TOTAL	$ 14,750.00

Linda Case and Victoria Downing,
THE REMODELER'S MARKETING POWERPAK,
Remodeling Consulting Services, Inc., 1995.

Finding an Enthusiastic Implementer

The most thoughtful marketing program is useless if it is not put into play. Who in your company is going to be responsible for seeing that your well-planned marketing activities happen on schedule?

Once the program is planned on paper, a creative, enthusiastic office manager can do it. Or you can find a good freelance subcontractor in your area who will see that the program is implemented and give you regular updates. Someone has to be responsible and consistent and committed. Don't miss this important key to your marketing.

Marketing Success Summary

A successful remodeler must emphasize value over price because a professional remodeler is never the cheapest. To spread this message about value a remodeler must become an aggressive and savvy marketer. Most remodelers could harvest many more leads and sales from their community with a carefully planned and organized marketing program. Here are the elements of a professional marketing program which will allow you to pick your clients, pick your jobs and achieve a good profit:

- Identify your prime customer and your prime type of job so the company can target its marketing to those prospects for those jobs.

- Fill a special need, a niche, so you can develop an excellent reputation as a specialist. People pay more to buy from a specialist.

- Target a realistic sales volume for the next few years so you can plan how many leads and jobs will be needed.

- Keep simple marketing statistics. Track and analyze the source of all leads and sales. Analyze close ratio—the average number of leads needed to produce one sale for the company.

- Qualify leads carefully to be sure that your sales time is well spent. Develop a profile of the perfect buyer and be sure that new leads fit this profile as closely as possible.

- Pursue referral lead sources aggressively by staying in touch with former customers and other referrers 3 to 4 times a year.

- Commit to customer satisfaction as the company's most important scorecard—as important as profitability.

- Market around jobsites with jobsite signs, vehicle signs, brochures, canvassing, and/or direct mail.

- Investigate home and mall shows as lead-gathering opportunities.

- Design your ads to target your prime customer, spell out the benefits to that customer, and ask for action.

- Evaluate each marketing tactic on the basis of how many sales it produces rather than how many leads.

- Develop a simple marketing plan each year and include some innovative marketing activity. The plan should build on last year's successes and drop marginal marketing activities.

- Evolve into a better and more effective marketer each year.

10

The Professional Sales System

Selling is a vital part of a successful remodeling business. The salesperson feeds jobs into the company, creating work and income for all of the other employees. A healthy sales record is a key step to the profitable future of a remodeling company. Without steady sales, your company is in peril.

As a remodeler, you're not selling a product—you're selling solutions to problems. You are in the service business and your job is to develop a solution that satisfies a client's needs at an investment that's deemed fair by both parties.

To be successful in sales, follow logical steps from start to finish. You may think, "Hey, I've been doing this for years by the seat of my pants and doing fine. I don't need a system." But, successful pros know that a step-by-step system makes a huge difference in effectiveness. If you're doing fine without a system, just think how much better you'll do if you follow one! A successful sales call follows a tried and true system like the following:

- Qualifying the prospect
- Building rapport
- Gathering information

☕ Presenting the company

☕ Presenting solutions

☕ Overcoming objections

☕ Closing the sale

☕ Follow up

Step 1: Qualify the Prospect

The best salespeople spend time at the beginning of a sales relationship to make sure that the prospect is a legitimate potential buyer for their services. Since your sales time is limited and precious, it's important that you don't waste any of it by dealing with prospects who clearly are not right for your company. Instead, use your lead form to find out if their project and your company are a fit.

Qualifying Leads

Here are some questions that will provide you with important information on the prospective client:

O   Is the prospect in the socioeconomic range the company desires? This information is often reflected by where they live and where they work.

O   Is the prospect interested in buying remodeling in a fairly reasonable time frame?

O   How did the prospect come to call this company? Most remodelers favor referral leads or previous clients over all other sources.

O   Does this prospect have a reasonable budget range in mind? This is a sensitive but important question to ask. You're simply trying to assess that the prospective buyer is in the budget ballpark. The lead may resist giving a budget range, in which case you should offer some ranges of similar jobs.

O Is this prospect in the geographic area you service?

O Is this a type of job you do?

O Has the prospect owned his/her house long enough to have built up significant home equity? This fact is considered an excellent sign that the owner is able to invest in remodeling.

O How much competition will you face? Statistically, bidding on a job with more than three other companies is a waste of time. Don't bother bidding against the unlicensed, uninsured carpenter/handyman. Explain to the prospect up front that you won't be the lowest priced so if price is the only issue, then you probably aren't the right company.

Most remodelers gather this important information and use it to make a spot judgment as to whether a particular lead is worth handling. If a remodeler has too many leads, qualifying is used to weed out poor-quality leads so they can concentrate on the best ones.

Using a lead form allows the remodeler to think out how the questions will be asked and to standardize the information-gathering process no matter who answers the phone. Every lead, even if it comes from a conversation at a church supper, should be tracked with a lead form. Only in this way can company data be maintained. Tracking competitive bidding gives contractors considerable insight into who their true competitors are, how their bids rank, and who they might refuse to bid against in the future.

SAMPLE LEAD FORM

LEAD FORM

Name _____

Address _____

Home Phone _____

Office Phone _____

Fax Number _____

Co-Owner' or _____

Spouse's Name _____

Address (IF DIFFERENT) _____

Jobsite Location (IF DIFFERENT) _____

_____

_____

☐ **Insurance Company:** _____

Adjuster _____

Phone _____

Agent _____

TYPE OF PROJECT

☐ Addition   ☐ Lower Level Finish   ☐ Custom Home   ☐ Dormer/Addition

☐ Kitchen   ☐ Porch/Deck   ☐ Commercial   ☐ Bath

☐ Siding   ☐ Windows/Doors   ☐ Interior Remodel   ☐ Tenant Finish

☐ Other

How long have you been considering the project?_____   Do you have plans? ☐ Yes   ☐ No

How long have you been living in this house?   _____   When do you hope to start construction?

Have you done any remodeling before? ☐ Yes ☐ No

If yes, did you: ☐ Do it yourself ☐ Hire a Professional ☐ Other:

If yes, is there anything you would have done differently?_____

If no, what concerns do you have about remodeling your home? _____

Can we be of assistance to you with financing? ☐ Yes   ☐ No

Are you familiar with our design/build process? ☐ Yes   ☐ No

What is your budget range? $ _____

HOW DID YOU LEARN ABOUT CCGI?

Previous Client (only)

Other Referral   Who?

Employee Referral   Who?

Insurance Company   Who?

Supplier   Who?

Arch/Eng/Designer   Who?

Comments: _____

_____

_____

_____

_____

Advertising

☐ Advertising

☐ Jobsite   ☐ Direct Mailings

☐ Vehicle Signs   ☐ HBA

☐ Yellow Pages   ☐ Horne Show

☐ Other: _____

Send: ☐ Letter ☐ Packet ☐ Folder

	TO DO	DONE
Mailing List	☐	☐
Remove From List	☐	☐
Sen LBQ:	☐	☐

Salesman: _____   ☐ Dead

CONSOLIDATED CONSTRUCTION GROUP, INC. in St. Louis, MO, gives top priority to the best leads. In order to rank the prospect, they use the following lead sheet for every telephone lead that comes in.

☞COACHING TIP

Some of the top selling remodelers chat extensively with the prospective client on the phone. These remodelers want to know a lot about the prospect's needs and wants—and even budget— before they commit to an appointment. The remodeler wants to walk into the first meeting with the right tools and samples and with rapport already established. One champion seller notes that he will spend 30-40 minutes on the first phone call to determine whether the prospect and his company are a good fit.

Once you've determined that the prospect is a qualified lead, it's time to make an appointment at the prospect's home to review the project. When you're making the appointment, be sure that everyone who will be involved in making the final decision will be present at your meeting. Ask the person to whom you're speaking, "Will anyone besides yourself be involved in making the decision to go ahead?" If they respond yes, ask that the other party be at the meeting as well. After all, you're trying to develop a solution that will please everyone and there might be questions brought up that you'd like to answer at the meeting. There's no point in your moving ahead with a solution if you don't know the needs and wishes of all involved parties.

Some remodelers use the time between the phone call and the appointment to send a letter confirming the appointment and a packet of company information to the prospect to pre-sell the company. This pre-meeting communication looks professional and helps the prospect become familiar with the company. After all, people tend to buy from people and companies they feel that they know.

Step 2: Build Rapport

Presenting a friendly, professional image is the next step in building a trusting relationship with your prospect. This first impression will set the tone for the entire relationship.

☞ COACHING TIP

Studies show that you have only 3 seconds to make that first impression—and then 30 more to turn it around if it was negative. Don't take chances with this all important first impression.

Be on time! Too many people take their customer's time for granted and show disrespect by showing up late—or not at all! You'll instantly set yourself up as a responsive, dependable company simply by showing up on time for your appointment. Call if you're going to be even five minutes late.

Dress professionally! The way you dress instantly conveys a particular image to the prospect, not only of you but of your company. Do you look like a professional? Or is your clothing wrinkled and soiled? Is your hair combed and neat? Or do you look like you need a haircut? Is your vehicle neat, clean and well-kept? Or is it dirty, dented and rusty? All of these elements affect the first impression. People want to buy from successful people so you have to look the part.

A rule of thumb when considering attire is to dress in the Sunday best of the people you're calling on. Therefore, if you're calling on blue-collar workers, khaki trousers and a neat polo shirt perhaps embroidered with a company logo would be appropriate for men. Neat slacks, blouse and a sweater or jacket would be ideal for women. Remember, if you look like a carpenter who just walked off the job, the prospect may perceive you as only being worth carpenter's wages. But if you look like a professional business owner or salesperson, they'll realize that they're dealing with a company that demands and deserves a professional wage.

VOICES OF EXPERIENCE...

Warren Kaufman, Renovations, Carmel Valley, CA, showed a focus group 12 pictures of himself in various types of clothing and asked "Which remodeler are you going to hire?" The final choice was Kaufman dressed in a blazer, dress slacks, dress shirt and tie.

From REMODELING magazine, May, 1997.

The best way to build rapport with the prospect is to start a conversation by asking thoughtful questions about their home, their history ("How long have you folks lived here?"), the neighborhood or something special about the home. It's also important to be courteous and attentive at all times.

Step 3: Gather Information

Buying is an emotional process rather than a logical one. Most people are buying your services to satisfy an emotional need which could be safety, comfort, status, or financial security. During this stage of the selling process, it's your job to

- discover the needs and wants of the prospect
- determine the priorities of these needs and wants
- have the prospect confirm these priorities

How well you gather this information will help or hinder you in creating the best solution for their problems. Since most homeowners talk to more than one remodeling company, the company with the best selection of services that develops the best solution to the problem will more than likely win the job. Listen carefully—gather the most comprehensive information you can.

The key to gathering pertinent information is to ask open ended questions—questions requiring more than a yes or no answer. This is the technique successful salespeople use to get in-depth information that may indicate uncovered needs or concerns.

OPEN-ENDED SALES QUESTIONS

? If you had the freedom to build whatever type of addition you wanted, what would you choose?

? Why are you thinking about remodeling?

? How long have you been thinking of this project?

? Tell me how you see the end result of this project.

? What happened to cause you to pursue remodeling now?

? What bothers you most about the home (building) you currently have?

? What do you like best about your home now?

? What difference are you looking for?

? How is your kitchen typically used? When does it seem most congested?

? How often do you entertain?

? What style of home do you like in general?

? How important is return-on-investment to you?

? What atmosphere do you want your home to have? Formal, casual, comfortable, clean?

? Have you remodeled before? How was your experience?

? What is important about the contractor you choose for this project?

By taking in as much information as possible and taking notes, you can refer back to them when you're presenting your solution at the next meeting. You might say, "You mentioned that you wanted to keep that oak tree on the south side of your yard but you also wanted to be able to capture more of the winter sun. Was that right?" The prospects will see that you were truly listening to their concerns. This is an important step in building rapport and trust.

Be sure to pin down a project budget at the first meeting. You may have tried to encourage the prospect to discuss this during your first contact, but now that you know the scope of work in more detail, you want to set clear expectations for the project cost before you move to design. If the prospects can't agree to a realistic budget range for the project, there's no reason to waste your time and theirs going further.

Using wide budget ranges as a discussion tool may help the owners determine what they want to invest. This method allows for some leeway if the owners make some changes. "Ballpark" budget ranges based on your history. For example, "We've done six kitchens in the last year and the investment has ranged from $10,000 for some cosmetic upgrades to $30,000 for a interior floor plan change, and new cabinets. With this project, a likely range would be from $20,000 to $25,000."

Often, remodeling salespeople make the mistake of assuming that they know what the prospect wants so they don't go back over the details with the prospects a second time to make sure. Instead, they find out when they come back to present their ideas and find out that they missed something important. Top salespeople confirm the details and the priorities before they leave the first meeting. At the end of the meeting say, "Now just to make sure I understand what you're looking for, let's just go over the details one more time, OK? Now, you've told me that... "

Review your notes with them again to make sure you haven't missed an important detail. Stop periodically to ask the prospects if you're on the right track. Let them confirm that you do indeed have it right. This will once again show the prospects that you were listening and that you consider their input very important to the process.

Step 4: Present the Company

Once you've gone over the needs of the prospect, take a bit of time to give them some information about your company and why you're different and a better choice than the competition. Be sure to focus on the aspects of your company that are most important to the prospects—information you'd uncovered earlier in the meeting.

Take sales tools to help you make your case for your company. People tend to remember information that they can see as well as hear. A presentation book is one of the most effective selling tools you have. Use an attractive artist's portfolio or binder and fill it with information about your company such as a copy of your license, insurance certificate, testimonial letters from previous clients, photos of past projects, customer and supplier references, reprints of articles your company has been featured in, community organization membership certificates (Chamber of Commerce, Rotary, etc.) and more. Remember, this is often the only concrete representation of your company the prospect will see. It should be organized, neat, clean and attractive as it's a representation of you and your company.

☞ COACHING TIP

As consultants, many of the presentation books we've seen were beautiful—in their day. Be sure to review your materials with a very critical eye every six months. Do the pages need replacing? Are the photos faded? Have the plastic page protectors become scratched? Does it need updating with fresh information?

A PROFESSIONAL PRESENTATION BOOK

Gerry Ellsbury, PLUMB SQUARE BUILDING GROUP, INC., Bethesda, MD, has created an attractive presentation book to help him walk his prospects through the services his company offers and differentiate his company from his competitors. These are several pages from his presentation book.

Full line remodelers usually need two or more meetings to sell the project. Specialty contractors are more likely to sell at the first meeting since they can price on site. If you are a full line remodeler, set up an appointment for the next meeting—within 7-10 days—before you leave the first. This forces you to move these prospects forward with momentum. Don't let the sales process drag.

Step 5: Present Solutions

If you have an attractive office, bring the prospects there for the second appointment. Exposing them to your territory shows you're stable and well-established. An office is a more controlled environment where you can hold a true business meeting without disruptions from children, televisions and phone calls.

Before showing the prospect your ideas, start by reviewing the overall strategy of the remodeling project—information that you and the prospect had agreed upon at the end of the first meeting.

Then show the prospects the sketches you've created or a detailed estimate that you've developed for their project. Increasingly, remodelers are using Computer Aided Design (CAD) or other means to create a visual selling tool to help close the sale.

☞COACHING TIP

Most prospects don't have the skill to visualize their completed project like you can. In many cases, even a floor plan is too abstract. Perspectives and elevations, no matter how rough, can help the prospect "see" your solution. The better they can imagine themselves living in their remodeled home, the more likely they are to buy.

VOICES OF EXPERIENCE...

Is it time to hire a salesperson to help you fuel the growth of the company—or to handle the sales function while you assume responsibility for other areas of the business? If so, here are tips for finding the right person from Bill Lee, president of Lee Resources, Inc., a Greenville, SC, consulting and training organization serving the building supply industry.

Top salespeople are "aggressive, competitive, and persuasive. These are folks who get right back up after they're knocked down. They have the mental toughness to deal with rejection. They have the conviction and the verbal skills to sell a reluctant customer or prospect.

"The best salespeople have a sense of urgency and a high energy level. Little grass grows beneath their feet. They're innovative and persistent. They know how to follow through. They live up to their commitments and achieve closure. They're relatively well-organized, or they're smart enough to team up with a sales coordinator who is.

"They're also attentive to details. They don't allow their fast pace to compromise accuracy. Too many mistakes are the undoing of even the most talented salespeople."

PROSALES magazine, August, 1997

Design Alternatives

Remodeling companies offering design capabilities are often known as design/build companies because they can handle the entire project from start to finish. Design is the first phase and construction is the second. This design capability could come from the owner and/or salesperson who has developed outstanding design abilities, or from an in-house architect. It could also come from outside resources such as a talented independent architect.

Offering design as a service creates one-stop convenience for your prospects. Design services can also differentiate your company from the competition. Also, when a prospect invests in a design created by your company, the chances of closing the construction portion of the sale are much greater. But remember, once you charge for design, your prospects are going to expect good design and comprehensive documents and drawings. Design/build—whether with an outside architect or in-house services—is a more customized and complex service.

In-House Design: Design/build companies typically charge the prospects a fee equal to 1-5% of the total construction budget. Sometimes the company will rebate part or all of this fee back to the prospect if their company is chosen to handle the construction.

Using an Outside Architect: Many remodelers who don't have an architect or designer in-house have developed a relationship with one or two independent architects who will handle the design of larger projects. Both parties understand that the lead belongs to the remodeler and both work to sell the job. The remodeler usually pays a reduced fee to the architect who acts as a member of their company team. This fee is then passed along to the prospect.

DESIGN LIABILITY

Structural failure due to inadequate design is not covered by normal liability insurance. A policy called Errors and Omissions does cover you but is prohibitively expensive and often not carried by design/build firms. Be aware of this potential liability. Be sure to discuss this problem with your local attorney before offering design services. Here are some tips for reducing your exposure:

- Develop designs with care and conservatism. Overbuilding is safer than underbuilding.

- Have drawings reviewed and stamped by a registered architect or engineer whenever doubtful.

- Schedule an opportunity for feedback from production managers and carpenters about design details to provide additional troubleshooting.

- Establish a clear agreement with customers that the design is only for the use of your company.

- Stamp this agreement on the plans and include it in any design contract. Some remodelers retain all drawings until the construction contract is signed, to be sure they will not be used by another contractor.

- If an outside architect or engineer is used as a consultant, obtain his/her insurance certificate and be sure he/she carries malpractice (Errors and Omissions) insurance.

As you review your proposed solutions with the prospect, pause regularly to ask if the prospects agree with the direction you're taking. During the discussion make notes on the changes they'd like to see. Only after you've completely discussed all of the details of the project do you present the investment.

COACHING TIP

Watch the words you use. During a presentation get "price" out of your vocabulary. Substitute "investment"—for that is what remodeling really is. Remove "bid" from your speech for it conjures up three contractors submitting competing prices and substitute "proposal." Consider using "client" in lieu of "customer." These are small but important changes that will set the tone for the sales call.

Once you've presented the investment amount, sit back, be quiet and wait for the prospects to respond. Don't jump in with conversation. This may be difficult, but wait for their comments before proceeding. Then, be ready to deal with their concerns and objections.

Step 6: Overcome Objections

A prospect's objection is one of the most useful tools in the sales process because it gives you additional information that allows you to move closer to the sale. A hidden objection is a roadblock to the sale but an objection brought out into the open where it can be addressed can be a stepping stone to a successful sale. The key is to be prepared for objections because they will come up! Be ready to respond and pull the prospect back into the selling process. Successful salespeople know that they don't give up when the prospect has an objection.

VOICES OF EXPERIENCE...

Gary Sannes, president of S.J. JANIS COMPANY, INC., Milwaukee, WI, has been selling remodeling for over 20 years, yet he never stops practicing his craft. Below is a crib sheet of common objections and responses that he carries with him and reviews before walking into every sales appointment.

The price is too high!

I can understand why you feel that way with the cost of products today. How does what we have proposed compare with your ideas? Budget? Goals?

We need to think about it.

What is it that you feel you need to think about? Have I been clear in explaining the project and our services? If I can help you to satisfy these concerns, would you be willing to move ahead— or are there other items holding you back?

We are getting more quotes.

Are you not pleased with our design? Budget? Products?
Price aside, do you feel comfortable doing business with us?
What have I failed to provide to you that you feel it necessary to talk with others?
There is obviously some aspect of my proposal that is not agreeable to you. Is it...?

Scheduling.

I understand that you are anxious to get started, but we need to properly plan and produce your job. Isn't that worth waiting for a few additional days (weeks) (months)?

> ### I'm not sure I'm ready.
> During my years in the home remodeling business, I have never heard clients say, "I wish we had waited until next year to do this remodeling project." But I've often heard them say, "I wish we had remodeled sooner so we could have enjoyed our room last year!"
>
> ### That's a lot of money to spend right now.
> Interest rates and construction costs usually go up over time. If you delay the job, it's likely to be more expensive.
>
> ### Undecided.
> Mr. and Mrs. Jones, we have something in common. You want a room addition and I very much want to build it. What do I need to do to get your business?

Step 7: Close the Sale

Once you've addressed all of your prospect's objections, it's time to ask for the order and close the sale. This is where many salespeople fail because they're not ready to handle the objection that they know will come up. But as a professional salesperson, it's your responsibility to ask for that order. Completing the sales process without asking for the order is like running a marathon without crossing the finish line. You've already done all of the hard work. Now it's time for the reward.

If the idea of closing the sale is threatening, just think in terms of asking the prospect to take the next step. What is the next step you want them to take—making selections, signing the design contract, visiting your office to review plans? Have the papers ready and presume the prospects will move forward. If for some reason they are not ready, go back to your questions to try to find out what is causing them to hesitate.

Buying Signals

Buying signals are clear indications from prospects that they are ready to buy. They begin thinking like clients and ask questions or make comments or take actions that should give you a strong message that it's time to move them into the purchase. Here's what to look and listen for:

Questions the client asks about the product or service

◄ How long will it take?

◄ How long will I be without my kitchen?

◄ Will your lead carpenter be on the job continuously?

Comments the clients make that indicate that they "own" the product mentally

◄ "I'll finally be able to find my clothes."

◄ "Maybe I'll get my closet back."

◄ "I won't be isolated in the kitchen anymore."

Actions the client takes that signify a buying orientation

◄ Relaxing.

◄ Taking possession of literature or plan.

◄ Reading specifications.

◄ Making notes.

◄ One spouse turning to the other and asking, "What do you think?"

Step 8: Follow up

Don't forget the client after the sale has been made, the contract signed and the deposit paid. They need reassurance that they haven't made a mistake. This trepidation comes in the form of the well known "Buyer's Remorse," something that happens to just about everyone after making a large purchase.

Immediately following the contract signing meeting, drop them a note in the mail thanking them for their business and reiterating the next step in the process. This will help ease their fears and reassure them.

WHEN THE PROSPECTS DON'T CHOOSE YOU

You'll often hear why customers chose your company. But you'll rarely find out why they didn't. To gather this information, send a short survey to all prospects who *didn't* buy from you. The responses will provide a wealth of information on your company's sales ability. For the best response, keep it short and include a self-addressed stamped envelope.

LOST JOB SURVEY

Thank you for the opportunity to consult with you on your remodeling project. It is important to us that we deliver the best service and highest-quality product available. If you would take a moment to tell us why you did not choose our company, it would greatly help our efforts to improve. Thank you. We appreciate your help.

1. Have you awarded your remodeling contract to another remodeling company? ☐ Yes

   Name of remodeling company who was awarded the job. (Optional)

   ☐ No. Please move to question 4.

---

2. Was your decision based on any of the following?
   (If more than one, please number in order of importance.)

   ___ Timeliness of response

   ___ Salesperson's ability to accurately assess needs

   ___ Company's ability to present creative solutions

   ___ Professionalism of presentation

   ___ Personal rapport with salesperson

   ___ Previous relationship with company

   ___ Product offerings

   ___ Company's reputation

   ___ Price. If price was a factor, was the estimate from our
       company higher by: ☐ 0-5% ☐ 5-10% ☐ 10-15%
       ☐ More than 15%   ☐ Other _____

3. How many times did you meet with the other company
   representative? ____

4 If you did not proceed with your remodeling project, why not?

   _____

   _____

   _____

   _____

   Would you like us to contact you in the future? ☐ Yes ☐ No

5. Please rate our company representative on the following:

Ability to listen and understand your needs

Poor 1   2   3   4   5   Excellent

Professional Appearance

Poor 1   2   3   4   5   Excellent

Presentation of company and proposal

Poor 1   2   3   4   5   Excellent

Technical expertise

Poor 1   2   3   4   5   Excellent

Quality of solution

Poor 1   2   3   4   5   Excellent

Timeliness of response

Poor 1   2   3   4   5   Excellent

Additional Comments: _____

_____

_____

_____

Remodeling Salesperson Job Description

Here is a sample job description for a remodeling salesperson used by one remodeling company. The duties vary from company to company. Responsibilities can include estimating, designing, and job production. Choose the combination of duties that works the best for you.

JOB DESCRIPTION—
Remodeling Salesperson

Overall responsibility is to sell remodeling projects to customers (homeowners) that meet the need of the customer, represent value to the customer and generate a profit for the company.

1. Dress: The salesperson will dress professionally. Minimum requirements for men are a pair of dress slacks, dress shirt and tie. The salesperson will present a neat appearance at all times.

2. Equipment: A late model car in good condition. This car will be kept clean and neat at all times. The salesperson must supply the following tools: *Clipboard, Regular cassette tape recorder, Calculator, Stepladder, Polaroid camera or 35 mm slide camera, Electric outlet tester.*

If necessary the company will purchase equipment and deduct from the first commission payment.

3. Hours: The salesperson is expected to work a minimum of (40) forty hours per week, making sales calls, prospecting for customers, and ensuring that jobs under construction are running smoothly. Because of the necessity for evening calls, the hours are flexible.

4. Responsibilities: The salesperson will be responsible for the following:

A. Maintenance of a company pitch book to be used during presentation to customers.

B. Maintenance of a company product catalog including up-to-date brochures and prices on all products.

C. Maintenance of company estimating manual and company price book with up-to-date changes as price changes are received.

5. Specific Duties

A. When a lead is received by the company a Sales Lead Card will be filled out for the salesperson. The salesperson's responsibility is to call the client to discuss the project and pre-qualify the client on the phone rather than waiting until the first appointment. The salesperson's responsibility is to arrive at the appointment on time, make a sales presentation and determine the customer's needs and desires. Once this is done, the salesperson will measure the job, using the room specification sheets and set up the second appointment to take place at the company's office. He/she will then estimate the job within two days. At the second appointment he/she will present the company's solution to the client, along with cost estimates of the project. Subsequent appointments will be as needed in order to sell the project or determine that the company has no chance to sell it.

B. *Project responsibilities:* Once a job is sold, the salesperson must submit a Project Binder which will include the following:

PURCHASE ORDERS AS FOLLOWS:
   a. Special Order Items
   b. All Subcontractors
   c. Complete Pricing

TOTAL ORDER SHEET

MATERIAL SELECTION/ALLOWANCE SHEET

JOB PLANS
Submit a design of the project that will include a scale drawing to 1/4" scale of all areas affected by the construction. This layout will include all details such as electrical outlet placement, door swings, and window locations.
Detailed Plans To Include:
   a. Floor plan with all correct measurements
   b. Cabinet layout with detailed drawings of
      any custom cabinets
   c. Elevations of all areas affected
   d. Necessary cross sections of specialized areas.

SALES NOTES
Room Specification Sheets
Conversation Notes

CHECKLISTS
Marketing Checklist
Pre-Construction Conference Agenda
Pre-Job Review Agenda

ACCOUNTS RECEIVABLE
Invoices

CONTRACT
Change Orders
Pre-Construction Conference Form
Contract

Job Costs
Production Management Report
Progressive Job Cost Analysis
Change Order Cost Report

C. Participate in the Pre-Job Review and Pre-Construction conference before the start of the work. At that time, specifications will be reviewed for the last time and all possible problems ironed out. Once that is done the production department assumes responsibility for completion of the job.

D. During construction, make at least three calls to be sure the job is running satisfactorily, maintain contact with the customer, and canvass the immediate area to see whether there are any jobs that can be obtained on a referral basis.

E. Be responsible for pricing and selling change orders over $1000.00 if they are other than routine changes that can be handled by the production department.

F. If problems arise during the course of a job due to interpretation of specifications, be responsible for working with the customer and production department to iron these out to everybody's satisfaction.

6. Commission Policy
The salesperson will be paid a commission on the following basis:
25% of actual (completed job) gross profit as long as the gross profit is above 35%. If the gross profit is 25-35%, commission will be 15%. There will be no commission on jobs with gross profit under 25%. Commission will be paid half upon signing of job and half upon completion and final job costing. Any pre-paid commission owed to the company must be paid back with next job.

7. Customer Service
The salesperson is responsible for calling customers back 30 to 40 days after final payment is received, to ensure that there were no problems on the job and that everything is satisfactory. Then the salesperson should ask for possible referrals for future work.

8. Product Knowledge:
Salespersons are expected to maintain their knowledge of products and keep up-to-date on current prices, new products introduced, and trends in the industry.

9. Sales Meetings:
Sales meetings will be held on a weekly basis on Wednesday mornings at 7:30am and it is the salesperson's responsibility to attend these meetings.

The Crucial Contract

No remodeling project should ever be started without a signed contract. A contract is simply a written and signed agreement between a remodeler and a client as to what will be done, how it will be done, when it will be done, how much it will cost and how that investment will be paid. Develop a standard contract which meets the requirements of federal, state, and local law. It should be a concise, simple document written in everyday language that's easy to understand. Your clients will appreciate the fact that you're not confusing them with paragraphs of "legalese." Before you use your contract, consult with your attorney.

Use your contract on *every* remodeling job because it protects both parties from misunderstandings and disagreements. After all, most people tend to remember negotiations in terms that are most favorable to them, so it's important to spell out the agreed upon work in writing—in detail—before the project begins. Take your time in reviewing the contract with the prospect. The time you invest in educating a consumer on how the business works and where specific responsibilities lie will be repaid by having the job run smoothly. In addition to your clients, insist that all employees be knowledgeable about the contract, the clauses, what they mean and how they are applied. Review your contract for needed revisions at least once each year.

☞COACHING TIP

It's not necessary to start from scratch when creating your company's contract. Use the resources available from the National Association of the Remodeling Industry, or the National Association of Home Builders. Also, several books have been published that contain pre-tested samples of contracts and other legal documents. Two of these are *Contracts and Liability for Builders and Remodelers* by David S. Jaffe, published by the NAHB's Home Builders Press and *The Contractor's Legal Kit: The Complete User-Friendly Legal Guide for Home Builders and Remodelers* by Gary Ransone, published by the Journal of Light Construction.

General Construction Specifications

Every contract should include detailed verbiage describing the project. Here is a checklist of common items that should be included in your contract:

- ✔ Permits and inspections
- ✔ Excavating
- ✔ Footings and foundation
- ✔ Termite treatment
- ✔ Rough framing
- ✔ Roofing
- ✔ Venting
- ✔ Gutters and downspouts
- ✔ Windows
- ✔ Doors
- ✔ Plumbing

- ✓ Electrical
- ✓ HVAC
- ✓ Drywall
- ✓ Ceramic tile
- ✓ Closet finish
- ✓ Interior trim
- ✓ Paneling
- ✓ Ceilings
- ✓ Painting and staining
- ✓ Finish floors
- ✓ Finish hardware
- ✓ Landscaping
- ✓ Carpet
- ✓ Walks and driveways
- ✓ Bath fixtures
- ✓ Kitchen cabinets
- ✓ Trash removal
- ✓ Jobsite cleanliness
- ✓ Dust protection

Your contract should include names of parties involved, job location, job specifications, a detailed description of the project, work schedule, payment schedule, and expiration of the proposal. In addition to these, include standard clauses such as:

○ **Warranty Terms:** How long do you warrant workmanship? Materials? This should be clearly stated to insure that clients cannot hold you responsible indefinitely. It should also make clear that the warranty does not begin until the project is substantially complete.

○ **Insurance:** Exactly what type of insurance will you carry and for what is the owner responsible?

○ **Dispute Resolution:** In the case of a disagreement, include a clause stating that you and the client will abide by the judgement of binding arbitration instead of a costly court solution.

○ **Hazardous Materials:** Spell out exactly what will happen if you discover pre-existing hazardous materials during the course of doing the project. Will you take care of it if you're able? If another company will handle it, who is responsible for hiring and paying this company? Will the job stop? What has to happen in order for work to resume?

○ **Change Orders:** Most remodeling jobs involve at least a few change orders to the contract and some jobs have many. Your contract should provide for change orders and describe how they will be handled. If you have an automatic administrative fee for each change order or if you require total payment of change orders upon signing, these requirements should be listed in the contract.

VOICES OF EXPERIENCE...

A well-written contract "allows you to take advantage of your years of experience in this business and communicate to the [client] how you want the business/legal aspects of the project to be handled. But there's a catch—you have to take the time and be organized enough to put the rules in writing prior to beginning the project. Now is the time to think ahead about what typical problems may arise...and how you would prefer to handle them. Then you can address these problems in the construction agreement you give the [client]."

Gary Ransone, THE CONTRACTOR'S LEGAL KIT: THE COMPLETE, USER-FRIENDLY LEGAL GUIDE FOR HOME BUILDERS AND REMODELERS, Journal of Light Construction, 1996.

Laws to Protect the Homeowner

Two federal consumer laws give homeowners 72 hours to cancel or rescind (terminate) certain transactions and require that consumers be advised in writing of these rights. Both laws should be included as a standard part of your contract.

The Right of Cancellation

This law gives consumers the right to cancel within 3 business days of the date of the transaction if (a) the remodeler personally solicits the sale, and (b) the contract is made in the consumer's home or a location other than the remodeler's place of business. Compliance with this law requires that you include a notice of cancellation clause in your contract.

Rules of Right of Cancellation

○ The buyer must be told orally at the contract signing that he/she has the right to cancel.

○ At the time of the contract signing, the buyer must receive a completed notice of cancellation, which must be (a) easily detachable from the contract and (b) set in type no smaller than 10-point boldface in the same language as that used in the contract and used in the oral sales presentation:

> You, the buyer, may cancel this transaction at any time prior to midnight of the third business day after the date of this transaction. See the attached notice of cancellation form for an explanation of this right.

○ This notice must already be filled out with the remodeler's name and address (the seller) and must contain the date by which the buyer may give notice of cancellation (not earlier than the third business day following the date of contract signing.)

The Right of Rescission

This law gives homeowners the right to cancel or rescind within 3 business days of the transaction if a security interest is taken in a consumer's principal dwelling and if the contract is considered to be financed (jobs with more than four payments). The consumer may exercise the right to rescind until midnight of the third business day following the sale.

Requirements of the Right of Rescission

You must deliver two copies of the right to rescind to each consumer. If two parties are owners (for example, husband and wife, father and daughter, or two sisters), each person must receive two copies of the right to rescind.

☞ The right must be presented as a separate document, not as part of a contract.

☞ It must identify the transaction.

☞ The right must disclose the security interest in the consumer's principal dwelling.

☞ It must inform the consumer of the right to rescind the transaction

☞ The consumer must be told exactly what procedure to follow to exercise that right and must be given the form for that purpose designating the address of the creditor's (remodeling contractor's) place of business.

☞ The consumer must be told the effects of rescission.

☞ The consumer must be told the date the rescission period expires.

Waiving the Right of Rescission

The right of rescission can be waived by a consumer's written statement only in a bona fide personal financial emergency. The statement must describe the emergency and bear the signature of all the consumers who signed the original contract. For example, this right might be waived to speed up emergency construction work that cannot wait.

Contact the Federal Trade Commission for a copy of these regulations.

Federal law is strict on how the contractor uses both of these notices. One or the other must be included in every remodeling contract, and they must be presented correctly. Develop the habit of complying fully with these requirements so that you don't have a slip up which could bring the weight of the law to bear on your company. It should be a standard part of your contract which has been reviewed by an attorney.

Invest in Professional Sales Skills

You can be a wonderful craftsman and an excellent design-er, but if you can't sell your ideas for a profitable investment, your other skills are useless. The successful companies of the future are going to be those who emphasize professional selling skills throughout the company. This is a crucial area for you and your team. Invest in developing a comprehensive selling system today and reap the benefits for years to come.

11

Estimating Accurately for Profit

The goal of estimating is to develop an accurate accounting of all of the costs of a project—including materials, subcontractors, and labor—then to use these costs as the basis from which to develop a sales price that will deliver a profit to the company.

It's your job as estimator to anticipate the project's cost as accurately as possible and to take into account everything that could cost time and/or money.

Estimating Methods

There are three basic estimating methods to choose from:

Guesstimate Method   **Stick Method**   **Unit Cost Method**

The remodeler using the **Guesstimate Method** for estimating uses knowledge of similar past jobs, basic intuition and on-the-job experience to take an educated guess at the cost of a project. This is certainly not a recommended method to use as it's just too easy make a mistake. While a very experienced remodeler may find himself guessing pretty accurately most of the time, he is bound to miss sometimes—and perhaps miss big. It's just too unreliable an estimating method to use exclusively. The only time an experienced remodeler may choose to use a guesstimate would be to orally provide the prospect with a preliminary budget range such as "This addition is likely to cost between $25,000 and $30,000."

The **Stick Method** of estimating lists all of the materials needed to complete the job, piece by piece, and each is priced individually. The subcontractors are contacted to provide a bid on the job and the hours of labor are calculated. Then, everything is added together to come up with the final cost of the job. The good side is that this method can produce very accurate estimates as long as all materials are included. The bad side is that if you miss one small element, your costs will be thrown off. Also, this method can be too time consuming to use if you are producing numerous estimates.

The **Unit Cost Method** relies on the cost per unit of measurement such as lineal, square, or cubic foot, or per item. All of the costs associated with the task are included in the unit cost. For example, the unit cost for installing a new window includes the window itself, framing material, nails, caulk and a factor for waste. A unit cost of labor is usually based on historical data—how long did it take a crew to complete a very similar project in the past?

VOICES OF EXPERIENCE...

Ed Castle, E.M. CASTLE CONSTRUCTION, INC., Silver Spring, MD says, "I started in this business without a great deal of history or experience so I purchased a unit cost estimating manual to help. But after using it and losing money on several projects, I realized that the information I was using did not accurately reflect my true costs. Now, I do stick estimates so that I'm sure I include everything—even though it takes a lot more time."

Estimating Systems

There are numerous tools available to help you develop accurate estimates using either the Stick or the Unit Cost method. These range from cost database manuals which contain hundreds of pages of prices for all materials and labor that may be needed in a remodeling job to elaborate computer software programs that integrate estimating with job cost reports and the company's monthly profit and loss statements. The manuals can be as inexpensive as $40 while the software can cost over $3000 for the program and up to three times as much for the training and support needed to actually use it.

Some remodelers have developed customized computer estimating packages that utilize their company's historic data for even more accurate pricing. While this can be very efficient, it can also cost a great deal to develop.

One of the most common estimating tools is the computerized spreadsheet. A spreadsheet can help insure accuracy by automatically completing the mathematical functions for you. Once the program is set up, it's just a matter of plugging in the numbers. Some remodelers still create their estimates by hand and then transfer the information onto a computerized spreadsheet for the final computations.

COACHING TIP

Unit Cost systems can be very efficient but they are rarely 100% accurate for any company. Top remodelers spend the time needed to customize the unit cost databases with historical data from their own company. Then they dedicate themselves to continually updating the database with new information. Once this is done, unit costing can be a quick, easy way to estimate.

ESTIMATING TERMS

Takeoff—The process of making a materials list using information taken from a set of plans, specifications, and inspector's notes. Figuring labor requirements of various trades may also be a part of a takeoff.

Direct Job Costs—Those costs that may be directly assigned to a particular job, usually wages plus fringe benefits for workers, material costs, subcontractors, plans, permits, fees, clean-up, and sometimes contractor financing costs.

Overhead—The general costs of running a business that cannot be assigned to a particular job, such as rent, telephone, office equipment and similar items.

Gross Profit—The difference between the selling price on a job and the direct cost.

Net Profit—The amount remaining when overhead is subtracted from gross profit on a job. Note that the owner's salary or wages have already been paid in overhead or direct job costs.

Markup—The amount or percentage that is added to job cost to produce the selling price. Markup must cover overhead and net profit.

Stick Estimate—A system for preparing estimates by preparing a complete materials list with required quantities for all the elements of a job, calculating the required hours and trades for labor, assigning a cost to all the items, and applying an overhead and profit percentage to the total.

Unit Pricing Estimate—A system for preparing estimates with costs based on units of measurement, such as square foot for walls and roof, lineal foot for footings or trim, and individual items for doors and windows.

Judgement Items—After the basic estimate has been made, the job must be analyzed for requirements such as specific job conditions, special features of the project itself, customer requirements, company capabilities and code requirements.

Specs—abbreviation for specifications, a detailed description (including dimensions, materials, products) for a proposed item of work.

Source: HomeTech Publications, Inc., Bethesda, MD

VOICES OF EXPERIENCE...

Randall Hall, RANDALL HALL DESIGN/BUILD, INC., Dallas, TX, knows that speed and responsiveness are keys to giving him a competitive edge, so he's developed a streamlined estimating system that helps him close sales.

"We don't spend time producing detailed, accurate estimates until we've sold the job," Hall says, "so we create a sales tool by using a broad brush approach to the project. By quickly plugging in numbers from similar projects into the 90+ categories on our customized spreadsheet, we can develop an estimate that's within 10% of the project's real costs. The spreadsheet automatically adds in markup, and creates a one page report with a range of high-medium-low prices that we present to the client. With this system, we never spend more than two hours estimating no matter how large the project."

Hall says, "It's a quick way to give the client the information they need to make an informed decision—and help us close the sale."

Standard Estimating Format

To consistently produce accurate estimates, it's important to use a standard format for every estimate. This format will list each phase of the project in the order in which it occurs—for example, it should start with plans and permits, followed by tear-out and demolition, excavating and grading until the project is completely estimated. By using this standard format, you're able to walk mentally through the process and include every detail in your estimate.

While you might have reworked figures several times during the course of developing an estimate, the final details and summary sheets should be clear and concise so that anyone would find the data easy to understand. In addition, a precise estimate with detailed, complete specifications can also be used as a production document for your carpentry staff.

Components of an Estimate

The majority of an estimate is made up of elements that create hard costs—materials, labor, subcontractors, and general expenses.

Materials—all items bought to install or use in a remodeling job comprise the materials for a job, including large items like lumber, doors, trim, fixtures, and small items such as caulk, nails, glue and other similar items. Too many remodelers lose money because they forget to add the small items into their estimate!

Labor—Labor is generally the most difficult area to estimate as it's a subjective call. Most remodelers will simply calculate the number of hours they think it will take a crew to complete a job. For example, if a remodeler estimated that their two-man crew could finish a project in 6 hours, that would be 12 total hours of labor.

This is multiplied by a predetermined figure to come up with the labor budget. However, the predetermined figure is not just the wages you pay to your field staff. In addition to the actual hourly wage, the labor figure should also include the *labor burden* which includes Workers' Compensation insurance, employer's Social Security contribution, federal and state unemployment compensation, vacations, holidays, health benefits, and other similar costs. This is usually expressed as a percentage of the hourly wage—25%-35% is a typical labor burden percentage. Since these are costs that are only incurred if the company has employees to do the work, they should be considered direct job costs. When they are included in the costs, these items are marked up along with the other direct job costs which increases your profit on the job.

VOICES OF EXPERIENCE...

"When estimating labor, be honest," says Jim D'Alessio, JAMES P. D'ALESSIO INC., BUILDERS, Deerfield, NH. "Don't cut back on the labor hours you've estimated in order to get a job. Be realistic. Remodelers tend to underestimate the time the job requires because they want to keep costs down to get the job. But that's an easy way to lose money."

Subcontractors—Subcontractors include the specialty trades such as plumbing, electrical, heating and cooling and masonry. Before the final estimate is delivered to the prospect, you should have written proposals from all subcontractors for the specific job. These prevent misunderstandings and spell out the responsibilities of each party such as who provides what materials. Often, subcontractors will provide standard prices for typical elements of the job allowing you to use these in the preliminary pricing stages. For example, an electrician may provide you with a set cost for installing outlets or light fixtures, heavying up the service, or similar tasks. But before the job is sold, the subcontractor should be asked to review the proposal by reviewing complete construction plans or, preferrably, by visiting the job.

General Conditions—For an accurate estimate, general conditions must be included as well. These could include permits, plans, dust and floor protection, rental equipment, temporary utilities, phone, and debris removal.

Judgement Factors—Now that the hard costs are estimated, it's time to take a fresh look at the project for other "soft" factors that may make the project more difficult. These could be

- *job related*—limited access to the job site, hard-to-match materials, extremely old building.

- *customer related*—needs a great deal of hand holding during the process, very picky about the condition of their home, looking for unrealistically high levels of quality.

- *or company related*—you already have a 4 month backlog and so can afford to raise prices slightly and take the risk you might lose this one project.

VOICES OF EXPERIENCE...

Sonny Lykos, THE LYKOS GROUP, INC., Naples, FL, says, "When you consider a job in terms of net profit amount instead of total sale amount, you'll be surprised at how your thinking changes. For example, an $8,000.00 job at an average 10% net profit suddenly becomes a $800.00 net profit job. Now, weigh that $800 bucks against the variables and other 'mitigating' factors you'll encounter, including the know-it-all neighbor or relative, argumentative spouse, and other loss generating potentials. Don't be like too many other contractors who, like I used to be, want every job and consider it an ego blow or personal insult if not selected. Be just as selective about whom you will work for as the owners are about whom they will hire."

Producing the Estimate

Accurate estimating is a result of a system that translates into habitual actions you take on each job you estimate. Those actions begin at the site and continue in your office to produce an estimated job cost you can count on.

At the job site,

☞ Walk the job with the customer (carry a clipboard, measuring tape, ladder, and flashlight). Make notes and take photographs of the existing conditions and areas where work will occur.

☞ Walk the job again, only this time alone. Use a checklist of existing conditions as a tool to help insure that you won't miss any detail. (See the example on page 215.)

Once back in the office,

☞ Put the exact specifications in writing. This is the only way that you or your subcontractors can estimate the job properly.

☞ If necessary, use allowances for any missing items or simply delete them from the proposal and make notes that they are not included.

☞ List judgement items and make decisions about how much to add to the estimate.

☞ Provide the major subcontractors with plans and a specification package to allow them to bid on the job. It's best if you schedule a walkthrough with them so they can see the actual job. That way you won't be hit with surprise extras later.

☞ Review the estimate carefully, checking and rechecking all mathematical computations, especially if you're doing it longhand. Even the most experienced estimators sometimes make mistakes. Using a computer spreadsheet or other estimating program speeds up the process and helps avoid these simple mistakes by handling the math automatically.

If possible, get second opinions from coworkers. A lead carpenter or production manager is an excellent person to double check your estimate.

COACHING TIP

To create accurate estimates time after time, develop some good habits right away:

✔ Choose a regular time to work on estimates. The best and most accurate estimates result from quiet, concentrated work.

✔ Work on only one estimate at a time. Trying to estimate several jobs at once is much too confusing and actually takes longer than working on one at a time.

✔ Estimate as soon as possible after gathering the facts. You'll remember more details, the customer will be delighted with the prompt response, and you'll show up your competitors who undoubtedly will take longer to produce their estimate.

INITIAL JOB VISIT CHECKLIST

Here is a sampling of common items to be considered in many remodeling projects. Use this "cheat sheet" to help you catch all of the conditions that affect the cost of the job. Only use the sections that pertain to the particular job.

Name: _____

Job Address: _____

Phone No.: _____ Fax No: _____

Availability of Owners: _____

Phone Calls Long-Distance: _____

Work to be Done: _____

EXISTING CONDITIONS
BUILDING—GENERAL

Style of House: _____

Stories: ____ Garage: ☐ 1 ☐ 2 car Finished: ____

Age (Approximate): _____

Construction: ☐ Wood Frame ☐ Brick/Stone

Bathrooms: (Qty)   ☐ Full   ☐ Partial

SITE

Access:

☐ Material Del. ☐ Excav. Equip. ☐ Concrete

Trucks

Driveway: ☐ Paved   ☐ Dirt

Lawn: _____

Well Location: _____

     Offset Line Location: _____

Septic System Tank Location: _____

     Field Location: _____

City Water/Sewer Line Location: _____

Place for Equipment Material Storage:

_____

Location for Dumpster: _____

Utilities:

☐ Oil (basement/underground) _____Gallons

☐ Natural Gas

☐ Propane Gas (above ground/below ground)

☐ Electrical Power Service
     (above ground/below ground)
     (with telephone and cable TV)

FOUNDATION: (Material used: Condition of)

Walls: _____

Frost Wall: _____

Crawl Space: _____

Slab: _____

Dampness: _____

Foundation Sealed: _____

FRAMING:

Sills: _____

Walls: _____

Subfloor: _____

Ceiling Joists: _____

Rafters: _____

Beams: _____

Sheathing: _____

Carrying Beams: _____

MASONRY:

Chimneys: Qty _____ Locations _____

Fireplaces: _____

Wood stoves: _____

Steps: _____

    Locations: _____

    Cement Brick _____

HVAC

Baseboard: _____ Radiant Heat

_____ Forced Hot Water

_____ Electric

Radiators: _____ Steam

Ductwork (Vents) _____ Forced Hot Air

Air Conditioning: _____

Domestic Hot Water _____

Boiler/Furnace Make: _____

Existing Zones: _____

    #1 _____

    #2 _____

    #3 _____

Gross BTU Output: _____

Net BTU Output: _____

Firing Rate: _____

PLUMBING:

Material: Supply (copper/galv./lead)

    Drainage (PVC / cast iron / copper)

Age: _____

Condition: _____

Faucets: ☐ Single handle Brand:_____

    ☐ Two handle Brand:_____

Tubs: _____

Showers: _____

Lavs: _____

Kitchen Sink:_____ ☐ Disposal ☐ DW

ELECTRICAL:

Service: 100/200 amp

    Spaces _____ Spaces Free _____

Material (wire) _____

Age: _____

Condition Circuit Breakers: _____

Switches/Outlets: _____

    Style: _____ Color: _____

INSULATION

Material: _____

Walls: _____

Ceiling: _____

WALL/CEILING FINISH:

Drywall: _____

Plaster: _____

Other: _____

TILE (other than floor): _____

EXTERIOR TRIM:

Rakes _____	Eave _____
Double _____	Double _____
Soffit _____	Corners _____
Frieze _____	Water Table _____
Molding _____	Porch Ceiling _____
Windows/Doors _____	Columns _____
Other _____	Lattice _____

ROOFING:

Shingles:

☐ Asphalt Color: ____ Brand: ____ Type: ___

☐ Wood Type: _____

☐ Slate Type: _____

Commercial Type: _____

Drip Edge: _____

    Eaves: _____ Rakes: _____

SIDING:

Material _____

Type:
☐ Clapboards ☐ Shingles ☐ Vinyl Siding
Other:

Finish:
☐ Painted ☐ Stained ☐ Other _____

Color: _____

Trim Color: _____

MILLWORK:

EXTERIOR

WINDOWS:
Manufacturer: _____
Type:
Frame: ☐ Wood ☐ Clad
Glass: _____
Grills: _____
Screens: _____
Hardware: _____

DOORS:
Manufacturer: _____
Type:
Frame: ☐ Wood ☐ Clad
Glass: _____
Grills: _____
Screens: _____
Hardware: _____

PATIO DOORS:
Manufacturer: _____
Type:
Frame: ☐ Wood ☐ Clad
Glass: _____
Grills: _____
Screens: _____
Hardware: _____

GARAGE DOORS:
Quantity: ___ Style : _____
Size: _____ Operators _____

INTERIOR:
DOORS:

Passage
Style _____
Material _____
Hardware _____

Closet
Style _____
Material _____
Hardware

Pocket
Style _____
Material _____
Hardware

INTERIOR TRIM:
Casings: _____
Baseboards: _____
Cornice: _____
Chair rails: _____
Stairs: _____
Closet Systems: _____
Finish: _____
Painted Color: _____
Stained Color: _____

STEPS/DECKS:
☐ Steps only _____
☐ Steps with Landing _____
☐ Covered Porch _____
☐ Deck _____

FLOORING:
☐ Wood Type: _____ Size: _____
Species: _____ Finish _____
☐ Carpet
☐ Vinyl
☐ Tile

OTHER
☐ Venting _____
☐ Bath Accessories _____
☐ Shower _____
☐ Gutter _____

APPLIANCES

☐ Refrigerator (free standing, built-in)

☐ Range: (Nat. gas, LP gas, Elec.)

☐ Cooktop: (Nat. gas, LP gas, Elec.)

☐ Exhaust

☐ Oven

☐ Microwave

☐ Dryer (Nat. gas, LP gas, Elec.)

SPECIAL ITEMS

☐ Security

☐ Central Vacuum

☐ Home Automated Systems:

Provided by Jim D'Alessio, JAMES P. D'ALESSIO INC., BUILDERS, Deerfield, NH

☞ COACHING TIP

One technique to help increase the accuracy of your estimating is to conduct a *job autopsy* after every job that does not come in on estimate—whether the cost is over or under estimate. Your goal is to be as accurate as possible so that you know how much each job will cost. When you conduct a job autopsy, you compare your estimated cost in each category with the actual cost to find the categories that did not match. By examining the reasons behind these discrepancies, you'll quickly learn how to modify your estimating system to become more efficient and reliable.

While there are numerous prepackaged estimating systems available, most remodelers have developed their own customized estimating system that combines some elements from these packages with their own particular methods. But, since it takes years of experience to be able to create an accurate customized system, an off-the-shelf package is a wonderful starting point.

No matter what system you choose, accuracy in estimating is crucial to the success of your company. A step-by-step system and a standardized format are the keys to the consistent precision that you must have.

12

Setting Key Production Goals

President Truman was known for the sign on his desk—*The Buck Stops Here.* In remodeling the buck stops at production. Any failure in your process at any stage shows up in production. Indeed production personnel often get the blame for a problem that might have originated in estimating or sales.

The emphasis, the respect and the attention that production is given in a remodeling firm primarily depends on how the owner views the importance of production. In some companies, the owner is sales oriented and may give short shrift to production. In most remodeling companies, the owner is completely production focused and may not value professional marketing and selling.

In both these situations, the company is unbalanced and in jeopardy. Owners need to realize that their company's success depends on successful marketing and sales *and* on the efficient delivery of the product.

Yet even where company owners are much too focused on production alone, the right things are not always targeted. Production often becomes firefighting—crisis management. Then schedule, budget and even customer satisfaction take a second seat to a disorganized use of resources thrown at a job that is already in trouble.

On paper, production's mission sounds deceptively simple. Production personnel just have to accomplish a three-part task:

Complete jobs on time,

within budget,

leaving a highly satisfied client.

But *simple* in this case doesn't mean *easy*. If your production department is not running as you would like it, start by reading this chapter. Then pass it along to each production person to read. Next hold at least three production meetings to discuss your company's position in each of the three major benchmarking areas—time, budget, satisfaction.

Let's review the systems for each of your goals and the reports you need to assess how those systems are working. Then we'll look at the team it takes to make those systems effective.

The Systems and the Reports

W. Edwards Deming, the revered business management guru, said that 85% of failures are the system and only 15% are the employee. Whether or not these percentages are exact, they target the importance of setting up a system focused on the results you want to achieve. You know the results you want—

jobs done on time

on budget

resulting in a happy client.

Deming also reminds us that when we have a problem, look first to the system since that is most likely where the problem lies. So that is where we will start.

Production Goal 1: On Time

Our On-Time Success goal is to have 90% of our remodeling projects completed on schedule. In Utopia (the perfect world), 100% of our remodeling jobs would be completed on or before schedule. In the real world, we might start with a goal of 85-90%. Remember the dictum:

You manage what you measure.

By measuring, we'll be able to improve our performance each year. But how will we measure this "jobs on time" performance?

👉 COACHING TIP

Linda Case advises "For the twenty-six years I've been working with remodelers, I have marveled at the lip service given accurate scheduling (a lot) versus the actual effort expended (not much). I vividly remember an experience I had five years ago while teaching a production seminar.

"A remodeler asked if he should go ahead and sign a contract that contained a penalty clause. The penalty clause said that if the job ran over schedule, he would be fined $50 per working day. The audience grumbled and fussed and remodeler after remodeler stood up to advise against signing such a contract. Then a remodeler in the front raised his hand. "I always make sure just such a penalty clause is in each of my contracts" he said. "That's the only way I can make myself serious about the schedule." Now there was a remodeler truly focused on schedule.

"As you can see, I never forgot that remodeler. I never forgot the lesson that when we are truly serious about something happening, we make it a priority and we monitor it."

Why do schedule overruns matter? For two critical reasons:

➤ **Jobs that overrun on time, overrun on budget.** Your estimate is timebased. Built into your estimate is a certain amount of overhead to handle the job. If the Harris job takes 6 weeks instead of three weeks, your personnel are there twice as long, the job requires twice as much overhead, and it takes you twice as long to collect your money.

➤ **Jobs that overrun on time leave clients unhappy.** Even if you can build a case showing the client how their decisions affected the deadline, they never really accept responsibility. Unhappy customers start to hold back money or make longer punchlists. The personnel who are stuck on the tardy job can't be earning money on the next job.

Commit to serious scheduling. There is no doubt that the real world conspires to make our jobs slow down. Homeowners are slow making a selection or deciding on an extra. Subcontractors don't work when they say they will. Suppliers are late shipping. But our job is to build in anticipated slack time and then keep the job moving as efficiently as possible during construction.

Scheduling

Since on-time performance is so important, base your commitment on the scheduling of each job and the commitment by all your staff (and the client) to the importance of that schedule. Remodelers most commonly use either a flow chart or a bar chart to schedule because they are easy to produce and easy to interpret.

A third method, the Critical Path Method (CPM), is often used in very large construction, but is utilized by very few remodelers because it is complex and takes more time to master. CPM is also less user-friendly in communicating with all the parties who help to keep the job on schedule. However, CPM is very effective in showing which tasks on the job are the most time sensitive ones (the critical path) as well as how various tasks are interdependent.

Flow Chart. A flow chart is a narrative schedule of what will happen on the job each day or each week. The advantages of such a narrative schedule are that it can include draws, reminders to order materials, subcontractor information, reminders to the customer, and potential snags. It is easily read and understood and takes no training to interpret.

Developing such a flow chart involves thinking through and planning changes in the production process to facilitate the job production schedule. By doing this strategizing you will already be facilitating the schedule.

JOB FLOW CHART

(Underscoring indicates that these items are to be done by someone other than the remodeling firm's employees.)

Week 1
<u>Client</u> to store furniture from addition
<u>Client</u> to remove items stored in two kitchen cabinets on back wall
Lead Carpenter (LC) to work out floor heights with owner
Install kitchen addition beam
Build wall security and install dust protection at the existing house
Demolish existing addition

Week 2
Cut in door between garage and basement
<u>Excavator</u>

Week 3

Basement windows needed

<u>Mason</u>—footings and foundation

<u>Inspection</u>—footings

<u>Wall check</u>

Week 4

Order rough carpentry materials

Backfill

Treat for termites

Tear off existing porch roof and reframe

<u>Mason</u> pours slab—Draw 2

Week 5

Rough carpentry—framing

Week 6

<u>Electrical</u> walk-through with owner to finalize decisions

Framing—Draw 3

Week 7

<u>Roofer</u>

<u>Mechanical</u> rough-in for electrical, plumbing, and HVAC

<u>Inspections</u>—mechanical

Draw 4

Carpentry—exterior trim and siding, cut through to house

Week 8

<u>Inspections</u>

<u>Insulation</u>

Carpenter—complete all rough framing, finish exterior

The Bar Chart. The bar chart is a graph with the tasks listed in chronological order down the left hand side and the days running across the top. Squares of the graph are filled in to designate when a task should take place. The Bar Chart is easily drawn manually on graph paper but not so easily updated. However, there are many inexpensive software programs that will produce schedules that are very simple to update as needed.

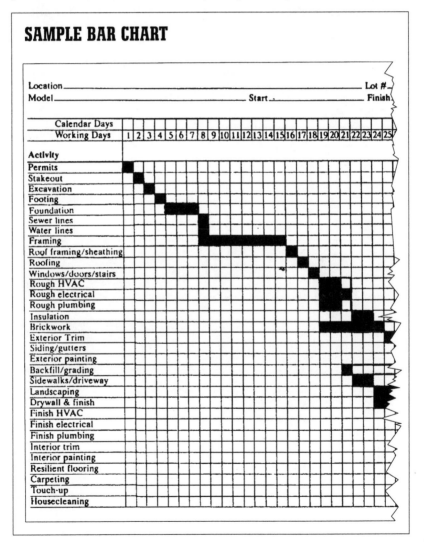

SAMPLE BAR CHART

Critical Path Scheduling. With CPM scheduling, the tasks that must be done on the days scheduled (or the project will overrun) are clearly shown. Tasks that have "float time" (or more days available to do the task than are needed) are also clearly shown. Thus, you know if you lose a half day in the first week from the critical path, you've lost a half day in the overall job unless you take some extraordinary action. However, learning to use CPM scheduling accurately and effectively takes training. And that training has to be extended to all of your personnel and subs.

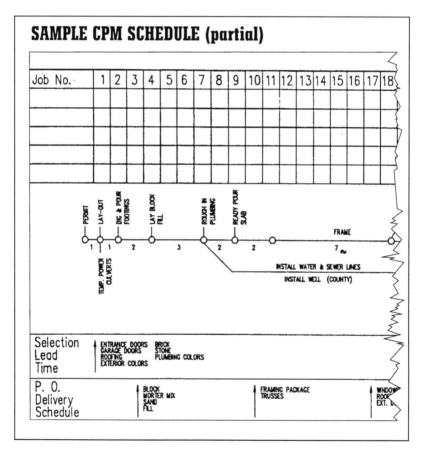

SAMPLE CPM SCHEDULE (partial)

Using Schedules

Scheduling is only worth doing if it is going to make a difference in how quickly the job runs. It is not like a football pool where you are betting on the outcome but cannot affect the outcome. Comprehensive scheduling should reduce project completion time significantly.

In order for scheduling to work in your company, the production manager and lead carpenter must commit themselves to the job schedule; they must refer to it and adjust it throughout construction. It provides a "map" of where the job is moving. It helps the company focus on the planning and adjustments involved in dealing with problems that impact the schedule. Scheduling is a crucial part of construction management.

When scheduling each week, the production manager should review the schedule for each of the individual jobs to see whether the jobs are on time, and if not, to see if any time can be made up.

The Benefits of Scheduling

Here's how jobs normally run without a schedule:

You start a two month job. Everyone feels there is plenty of time. Decisions are made daily to move people, to let a sub go to another job instead of this one. There is no client pressure because rough framing goes so quickly that they think you are ahead of schedule. The client makes changes, is slow to make selections, but is never made to feel concerned about time frame. About the time you finish drywall and begin trim, you begin to notice that the remaining time is impossibly short. But at this point it is too late to pick up any significant time to reclaim your original completion date. The job, the budget, the client are all beginning to fall apart.

Here's what happens when you schedule effectively. Let's take the same job. You are into your second week and doing roof sheathing. Since you review the schedule at least weekly, you see that you are 1/2 day behind so you quickly reshuffle carpenters and the electrical sub, and work out a way to pick up a 1/2 day. Voilá, you are back on schedule.

There are many benefits to accurate scheduling:

 You'll be able to predict cash flow from draws and payables.

 You'll know when you need personnel on the job.

 You'll be able to let subs and suppliers know far in advance when materials or mechanics will be needed.

 You'll be able to tell new buyers when their jobs are likely to begin.

 You'll be able to sell and document your company's commitment to on-time delivery.

" VOICES OF EXPERIENCE...

Allen Zaring of ZARING HOMES in Cincinnati is reducing. Not weight, but the company's "cycle time." He wants to reduce the time it takes to sell and build a home from 152 days to 60. He's now at 128 days and counting.

"This industry is obsessed with cost-cutting by squeezing subs and suppliers," says Zaring. "It creates adversarial relationships between the builder and the vendors. We're obsessed with cycle time reduction. Not only will it yield better results, but it's free. It doesn't cost anybody a penny."

BUILDER magazine, 8/96

How to Schedule Successfully

Here are eight techniques for successful scheduling:

O   Be optimistically realistic. It is likely to take your company a year to learn to use schedules effectively. You will be too optimistic at the beginning. Jobs get done very quickly on *paper!* Good scheduling means leaving enough open time but not too much. One remodeler leaves 1 1/2 days of each week unscheduled to allow for bad weather, late deliveries, no-show subs or labor that's running behind. This may be too loose or too tight for your company (and the weather in your region).

O   Everyone whose work is governed by the schedule should have some input. You want these people to "buy in." You won't have that as long as the schedule is imposed on the worker. In particular, the lead carpenter should help in the development of the schedule. That way, they understand all phases of it and will be much more likely to take it seriously.

O   Remind everyone when draws are due with regular notations on the schedule.

O   Add time to the schedule for change orders. Thus the change order might say at the bottom "Changes extend completion. Please add three days to the schedule if you approve these changes."

O   Review the schedule every few days with the lead carpenter and review it again in the weekly production meeting. Only by this constant checking does everyone stay focused on what is important.

O   When job timing starts to slip, get everyone involved in how that time can be re-won. Personnel will see how serious you are about on-time performance by how hard you fight to make up lost days.

○ Some computerized programs make it easy to update the schedule but obliterate the original (desired) schedule. Instead, you need a program that shows the original schedule as well as the revised schedule to allow you to compare the two.

○ When jobs are complete and are reviewed for profitability, they should also be reviewed for maintenance of schedule. Some remodelers give the field personnel a bonus if the job comes in on time. That bonus might be $250 on a $25,000 job.

Punchlists and Schedules

Include completion of the punchlist in your schedule. That last two percent of the job often takes it way over schedule—and budget. You worked so hard to achieve customer satisfaction during the first 98% of the job—you don't want to lose it in the final 2%!

Your On-Time Reports

On-time performance should be measured on each individual job and that is handled through the individual job schedules. You want to track the quarter's jobs as a whole or the year's jobs as a whole. Only then can you measure progress and will you be able to say, "Last year 76% of our jobs completed on time and this year—to date—82% are on-time." That report can be called your On-Time Summary Report.

Production Goal 2: On Budget

Our On-Budget Success goal is to have average actual job costs within 2% of estimated. Again in Utopia—that perfect world—every job would come in at or under budget and that is our goal in remodeling.

The first task is to establish the budget for each job and then for all jobs as a whole. Your job estimate is the budget for the individual job cost. The company's annual financial budget is the estimate for the company as a whole. This budget estimates a percentage of income for job costs. That percentage is directly related to markup as we learned in the financial section. For example, if you use an across-the-board markup of 50% on your jobs, your job costs should run 67%, leaving 33% for your gross profit.

Your second task is to measure the actual results on each job. As discussed in Chapter 6, that's why job cost reports are so critical. Many remodelers share estimates with lead carpenters and production managers and get their help in the tough task of keeping jobs on budget.

Bringing Job Costs as a Whole in on Budget

You'll track individual job costs. And it is critical that you do. But what does your mind do with the information that the $10,000 Harris job was 7% under budget and the $3,000 Jones job was 12% over and the $40,000 Simmons project was 2.5% over and on and on and on...? Truth is, your mind can't process a bottom line from so many bits of information.

So how do you know how the totality of your jobs are doing? Are they producing the gross profit you need to run your company? That's the important overall issue for you to monitor. Yet that measurement is rare in companies. We could call it a Summary Job Cost Report. Following is an example.

SUMMARY JOB COST REPORT

JOB NAME	JOB TYPE	SOLD BY	AMOUNT OF CONTRACT	EST. SQS.	ACT. SQS.	+ / – SQS	COST OF DIFF.
Carr	R	D	$ 4,500.00	24	24	0	$ 0.00
Reid	R	D	11,900.00	141	135	0	528.89
Black	W	D	2,750.00	11	11	0	0.00
Simms	Trim	M	1,491.00	1	1	0	0.00
Barry	W	M	1,435.00	2	2	0	0.00
Kreiser	R	D	3,625.00	28	27.7	.3	44.56
Pully	R	D	1,550.00	15	15	0	0.00
Garrett	W	D	2,400.00	1	1	0	0.00
Simpson	L	D	975.00	138	138	0	0.00
Oliver	L	D	840.00	143	151	-8	(44.50)
Downs	L	D	1,168.00	183	183	0	0.00
Hess	L	D	1,800.00	325	325	0	0.00

| Summary | | | $ 34,434.00 | | | | |

COST OF MATERIAL	COST OF LABOR	LABOR PER UNIT	TAX ON LABOR	DUMP & MISC.	GROSS PROFIT	% GROSS PROFIT
$ 851.04	$ 1,555.00	$ 64.79	$ 93.30	$ 450.00	$ 1,643.96	37 %
4,462.49	1,469.00	10.88	88.14	—	5,968.51	50 %
1,427.30	117.00	10.64	7.02	258.00	947.70	34 %
524.01	503.12	503.12	30.19	90.42	373.45	25 %
645.64	68.75	34.38	4.13	—	720.61	50 %
1,021.18	434.00	15.69	26.04	200.00	1,969.82	54 %
504.35	279.00	18.60	16.74	—	766.65	49 %
1,123.32	305.25	305.25	18.32	108.00	863.43	36 %
186.69	60.00	0.43	3.60	35.60	692.71	71 %
173.12	65.00	0.43	3.90	34.40	567.48	68 %
368.66	134.50	0.73	8.07	43.60	621.24	53 %
452.84	312.50	0.96	18.75	95.20	939.46	52 %
					$ 16,075.02	47 %

Linda W. Case, *The Remodeler's Guide to Making and Managing Money*,
Remodeling Consulting Services, Inc., 1996

This report shows you the pattern of your jobs as a whole. You don't get that information anywhere else. With the help of computer sorting, this report can allow you to gather some very valuable information -

If I sort the jobs by job size, are some more profitable than others?

If I sort the jobs by job type, are some more profitable than others?

What if I sort by salesperson?

What if I sort by lead carpenter?

Being able to sort data in this way will give you the precise information you need to make important decisions such as to let personnel go, change your market niche or change your markup based on job size or job type.

Because you need completed jobs for the Job Cost Summary Report, most companies update it quarterly rather than monthly. It's probably best to focus on your targeted gross profit percentage because that will be easier than targeting the dollar numbers in the original estimate which will have to be updated with each change order.

JOBS REPORT BY PROJECT TYPE

Project Type:	# of	%	Total Value:	%	Average Job Size
Awnings	9	4.3%	$19.459.00	1.2%	$2,162.00
Bathroom Remodel	8	3.8%	44.159.69	2.7%	5,519.00
Carport	1	0.5%	3,800.00	0.2%	3,800.00
Commercial Remodel	2	1.0%	35,800.00	2.2%	17,900.00
Decking	2	1.0%	11,685.00	0.7%	5,842.00
Doors - All Types	14	6.7%	18,380.00	1.1%	1,312.00
Flooring - All Types	1	0.5%	816.50	0.0%	817.00
Gazebo	1	0.5%	4,000.00	0.2%	4,000.00
Gutters, Fascia, Soffit	3	1.4%	1,175.00	0.1%	391.00
InsuranceWork	14	6.7%	36,485.13	2.2%	2,606.00
Kitchen Remodel	2	1.0%	52.525.80	3.2%	26,262.00
Miscellaneous Carpentry	15	7.2%	28,922.50	1.8%	1,928.00
New Homes	1	0.5%	220,000.00	13.4%	220,000.00
Painting/Wallpapering	5	2.4%	9,879.00	0.6%	1,975.00
Patio Enclosure Addition/Cover	9	4.3%	127,149.00	7.7%	14,127.00
Roofing/Roof Repairs	48	23.1%	275,919.30	16.8%	5,748.00
Roorn Addition	5	2.4%	222,904.00	13.5%	44,580.00
Room Conversion	2	1.0%	12,480.73	0.8%	6,240.00
Room Modification	2	1.0%	1,465.00	0.1%	732.00
Siding - All Types	35	16.8%	292,681.00	17.8%	8,362.00
Whole House Renovation	3	1.4%	125,313.00	7.6%	41,771.00
Windows	26	12.5%	101,209.32	6.1%	3,892.00
Total:	208		1,646,208.97		7,914.00

While this company has an average job overall size of $7,914, its jobs actually range from an average of $220,000 per new home to $391 for gutter jobs. The owner has information in this report to see the types of jobs, average job sizes and the contribution of each type of job to the overall volume.

Who Cares about these Job Cost Reports?

You, the company owner, care and should receive at least biweekly reports on how the individual Job Costs are coming in and a monthly Summary Job Cost Report on the profitability of the jobs as a whole.

The Production Manager cares because his/her job is to monitor and correct any problems in our "on budget, on time, with a happy customer" system.

Each lead carpenter cares because he/she knows that monitoring and managing time favorably affects costs on his/her job. The lead receives and monitors the bi-weekly ongoing job cost vs. budget to see how his/her job is progressing.

Everyone in your company cares because they all want the job security that on-budget production brings.

☞ COACHING TIP

90% of job cost overruns are in labor—the riskiest of the cost categories. So why not subcontract as much of the job as you can? Don't have your employees do insulation, roofing, drywall. Get fixed prices for those areas of the job and sleep better at night.

Production Goal 3: Leaving the Client Happy

Our third goal for the successful delivery of the remodeling project is leaving a delighted client. We might quantify that to say we want to be rated 9 or 10 (on a 1 to 10 scale with 10 being excellent) by 90% of our clients.

So how can you get that high rating? If you ask a remodeling customer what they want from their contractor, they are likely to say that they want their job done:

- on time,
- on budget—with no surprises, and
- with sensitive attention to their needs and concerns.

Notice how these wishes mirror your wishes as a remodeler. So by focusing on the three production benchmarks, you will go a long way toward making money and having satisfied customers. Who says you can't have it all?

Why Client Happiness is Vital

Your customer's level of satisfaction is critically important for three reasons:

1. Unhappy customers bleed the company of profit. No matter how high the level of markup, the ability of an angry or unhappy customer to pull a job into red ink with lengthy punchlists, reworks and hassles is greater.

2. Unhappy customers don't refer those high-quality new leads to you. Surveys show that the unhappy customer tells twice as many people about how your company fell down on the job than the happy customer tells how much they liked your company.

3. Unhappy customers are destructive to the morale of your employees and subs. Most people attracted to working in a service business truly want to serve and please the client. By its nature, remodeling involves a long-term relationship with your buyer, and living through an unpleasant job can be an extremely difficult and demoralizing process.

 COACHING TIP

Remodelers often ask whether they should add to the sales price of a project to compensate for the fact they believe a potential buyer will be a difficult client. We recommend not selling to this client. There is no amount of money worth the hassle to you and your subs and employees and there is no amount of markup large enough to assure that you won't lose money on the job with this client. Run, don't walk, from this prospect.

What Do Customers Want?

While you must work to discover each individual's special needs and "hot buttons," many elements of customer concern are known. Here are seven universal wants:

- Customers want you to be an expert. They want guidance in their buying decisions. They want to be assured that the new space will be structurally sound, well-crafted and well designed. They want the remodeler to provide expert suggestions regarding product selections.

- Customers want you to be trustworthy. Unless mutual trust develops between you and the client, the project is doomed. A well-written contract provides an excellent legal cushion on which to fall back, but nothing substitutes for two parties who respect and trust one another.

- Customers want you to deliver what is promised. They don't want to be a supervisor whose job is to catch you doing things wrong. In fact, most clients today do not have the know-how to police their jobs. This puts a burden on you to be sure sales approaches, contracts, and change orders are all as clear as possible and that they spell out the nature of your work in terms that any lay person can understand.

- Customers want you to keep them informed about what to expect next, what has been done, and how the schedule is progressing. Remodeling is an exciting and somewhat frightening prospect to them and most customers can deal with the ups and downs if they have honest information.

- Customers want to be assured that their job is important to the company and that they will receive top priority treatment.

- Customers want you to be sensitive and considerate about their living conditions. They want cleanliness, neatness, and their home and yard to be treated with care.

- Above all, customers want you and your personnel to be friendly, optimistic people. They don't want to hear why something can't be done. Instead, they want their needs and desires to be approached with a "can do" spirit whenever possible.

Measuring Client Satisfaction

Since you manage what you measure, develop a system for measuring client satisfaction during the job and after the job. While construction is ongoing, regular weekly meetings with the client can be your most effective tool in checking their mood. But have you ever noticed that if you ask your client "How's everything going?" you're likely to hear "Fine," whether it is or not.

To hear the real story, an Oklahoma remodeler asks the client to rate their satisfaction level on a scale of 1 to 10 with

1 being "ugh" and 10 being "great." Using this quick and easy test elicits a more thoughtful reply. If your score is below 9, find out why and what you and your personnel could do to improve.

Determining your client's overall satisfaction level at the end of the job is easier. Many remodelers mail out an evaluation form with a stamped, self-addressed envelope for the client to fill out and return. By making the evaluation numerically scorable, you will be able to check the overall satisfaction level of all your customers from year to year.

CUSTOMER EVALUATION

Name (Optional)

As you circle your ratings, please remember that a "5" rating is excellent; a "1" rating is poor.

	Poor			Excellent	
1. How happy are you with the project design?	1	2	3	4	5
2. Was our salesperson courteous and helpful?	1	2	3	4	5
3. Was the design process smooth?	1	2	3	4	5
4. Was our salesperson knowledgeable?	1	2	3	4	5
5. Was our office staff friendly and efficient?	1	2	3	4	5
6. Were we accessible when you phoned, and timely about returning your calls?	1	2	3	4	5
7. Was our production manager responsive to your concerns and questions?	1	2	3	4	5

---

8. How would you rate the people working   1   2   3   4   5
on your job?

9. Were our subcontractors professional and   1   2   3   4   5
quality conscious?

10. Did we clean-up as expected?   1   2   3   4   5

11. How was our overall performance?

_____

_____

12. What did you like best about working with us?

_____

_____

_____

13. In what areas should we concentrate our efforts to improve?

_____

_____

_____

14. Additional comments. (If you rated us poorly on any section, we'd appreciate any specific comments you might have relating to our performance in that area.)

_____

_____

_____

15. Do you know a friend, neighbor or business associate who could benefit from our services?

_____

_____

_____

Optional

Name _____

Address _____

City/State/Zip _____

Thank you!

Linda Case and Victoria Downing,
THE REMODELER'S MARKETING POWERPAK,
Remodeling Consulting Services, Inc., 1995.

VOICES OF EXPERIENCE...

Larry Parrish, R.C. PARRISH COMPANY, INC., Boulder, CO, has an independent public relations firm mail his Customer Satisfaction Survey to assure his clients that they can be candid. Clients who return the survey are offered a free subscription to their choice of a national remodeling magazine or a Colorado home-focused publication.

Achieving Production Goals

You're focused on the three critical goals of production (on time, on budget, with a high level of customer satisfaction) and how to measure your achievement of these goals. Now let's explore the production team and the revolutionary changes the industry is making in job responsibilities. Then we'll walk through the key steps your production system should include.

13

Marshaling Your Production Team

There's been a quiet, yet powerful revolution in how production is handled in many of the most successful remodeling companies. This revolution is most evident in the changing job descriptions of the carpenter and the production manager. These changes are powered by the new quest for quality in all of American business, often coupled with the search for a streamlined organization.

The traditional view—Work was done properly only if personnel were heavily supervised. The carpenter on the job was responsible only for the carpentry. The superintendent was primarily a checker, supervisor and babysitter who tried to get to each job each day and right those things going wrong. Materials and subs were centrally ordered and tracked by the office. The carpenter was encouraged to have as little contact with the client as possible. Yesterday's superintendent could oversee approximately $600,000 in volume annually.

The new view—All systems are aimed at getting the job done right the first time by the front line worker. The carpenter on the job is not only responsible for the carpentry but also for the management of that job and the resources (subs, materials) needed to do it. The production manager is an expeditor for the front line who spends much less time "supervising" and a great deal more time facilitating, coaching and training. The production manager is responsible for seeing that the jobs come in on time, on budget and with a satisfied client. Because of this change in job description, today's production manager can oversee approximately $1 million to $1.5 million in remodeling volume annually.

All production staffers have taken on more management and more responsibility. There is less supervision needed and given. Let's look at each position within a production department.

The Lead Carpenter

The term *lead carpenter* designates the working head carpenter in charge of a job. Increasingly, the lead carpenter is charged with greater management responsibility. In addition to performing the carpentry work on the job, this responsibility could include:

☞ Monitoring job costs, especially labor, against estimated costs.

☞ Day-to-day material takeoffs and orders.

☞ Scheduling subcontractors once their contracts are approved by the production manager.

☞ Managing all labor at the jobsite including subcontractors.

☞ Front line responsibility for customer satisfaction.

Developing a staff of top lead carpenters should be a long term goal for your company. This job demands a diverse group of skills and many carpenters neither want to assume the task nor have the ability to carry out the role. Examine the benefits — real and psychic—you offer these key employees and be sure that you have a quality package to attract and retain superior leads.

Hiring Outstanding Lead Carpenters

In many parts of the country, hiring a well-qualified carpenter with a positive attitude has become an extremely difficult task. The boom in general construction, the decrease in the population in the 18- to 25-year age range, and a lack of interest in manual labor among the young have combined to make finding this key person more and more difficult. Here are eight ideas that may help you with your search:

— Advertise in the classified section of the newspaper, but do not assume this is the only way to find a new employee. Spend some time writing an ad that really states what the company wants and the benefits you offer. Use more space than the surrounding ads use. Request that applicants send or fax a letter or resume and then set up a thoughtful screening program for respondents.

— Tell everyone you know that the company has an open position for an outstanding carpenter. Offer a $250 bonus to the employee who refers a lead carpenter to the company who is still on board three months after hiring.

— Put flyers in employee paycheck envelopes, notify suppliers, post notices on all available bulletin boards. Let fellow contractors know by inserting a note in the local industry association newsletter.

— Find ways to reach the *employed* lead carpenter rather than those who are unemployed. Classified ads in industry publications may be more productive than the general newspaper. Consider placing flyers on cars and trucks at the local lumberyard, hardware store or building supply store, but check local laws on distributing handbills first. A permit may be needed.

— If the usual recruitment methods do not work, try something unique. One company provided their suppliers with notepads to give to their customers. The pads included a recruiting message for the contractor.

— Consider inviting carpenters to an evening open house at the company office. This event allows carpenters to drop by after work to look the company over. Have your personnel in attendance. Serve pizza and soda and sell your company benefits.

— Don't overlook the self-employed carpenter who may decide the hassles and uncertainties of business ownership are not worth the trouble. These people make wonderful lead carpenters because they understand the entire business.

— Be aware that outstanding carpenters are in demand and, therefore, can pick their jobs. Write up a list of benefits (health insurance, little down time, four-day workweek, jobs that call for great craftsmanship, award-winning projects) that you offer. Consider the search for a top employee as a marketing effort.

☞ COACHING TIP

We are often asked how much a lead carpenter should be paid. Only you—in your exact locale knowing your local economic conditions—can judge that. Pick up the Sunday classifieds and start answering ads as though you were an applicant to see what is being offered. Be aware that top lead carpenters usually earn $4,000-$8,000 more annually than the ordinary carpenter.

The Lead Carpenter Job Description

Overall Responsibilities:

Customer Satisfaction
Carpentry Labor
All Subcontractors
All Materials
All Inspections
Collection of Progress Payments
Job Clean-Up
Completion Date as Specified
Maintenance of Job Records

Specific Duties:

1. You are XYZ Construction's on-site manager of the construction job. Your good performance is extremely important to the success of our company. You are on the 'front line' in achieving our company goals of superior product quality and superior customer satisfaction.

2. You are responsible for knowing and understanding all job paperwork: plans, specifications, and change orders. Any question you have, or discrepancies you discover, should be checked with the production manager.

3. You will participate in the pre-construction conference and the quality control pre-completion punchlist, along with the production manager and customer.

4. You are responsible for performing all carpentry labor on the job, requesting help as it is needed. When other carpenters or helpers are on your job, you are responsible for assigning them work, expediting their performance, and generally supervising them.

5. Time cards for all personnel should be checked by you for accuracy, and signed and turned over to the production manager by noon on Thursdays. No checks will be issued without a time card.

6. You coordinate all subs, work out their layout problems, ensure their proper performance, and approve their payment, as well as seeing that they get timely inspections on their work.

7. You are responsible for ordering materials promptly and accurately, with at least 24 hours notice. Please be sure to check material deliveries for accuracy in quantity and measurement, and for any quality problems or damage. Truck drivers are to wait for your inspection, because when you sign their delivery ticket you are saying there is no problem with the delivery. Be sure to note any problems right on the ticket. Job personnel should pick up materials only under emergency conditions.

8. Protect the customer's property. Do not use, or allow others to use, any of the customer's equipment, tools, or cleaning supplies.

9. Set up and monitor a 'safeplace' on the job where items to be reused are protected.

10. You are responsible for the customer's security. Be sure to lock up carefully at the end of each day. Do not leave ladders at house windows for possible use by burglars.

11. Adequate dust protection is one of your most important jobs. Try to keep all dust and dirt as isolated from the customers as possible. Broom-clean the job site daily, and see that trash is hauled at least weekly. Trash should be put on plastic that is laid on top of plywood. Absolutely no food trash is to be put in the construction trash. Put all food trash into the customer's trash cans.

12. Deliver customer invoices and collect progress payments according to the contract terms.

13. Smoking is not allowed inside any of our projects. Outside, see that a butt can is designated and used if there are any smokers on the job. No abusive or foul language is to be tolerated. Radios should be played quietly. Absolutely no alcohol or drugs may be used on the job or anywhere near the job site, even outside working hours. Such use of alcohol or drugs will result in instant dismissal.

14. The customer's telephone should be used only for business or emergency personal calls.

15. If the customers wish to make changes or have extra work done, please be sure to refer them to the production manager.

16. Be responsible for installing a job sign in the most prominent place, and keep it in good condition.

17. Be sure the job stays on schedule or ahead of schedule by monitoring progress on the flow chart. Notify the production manager if you will have any problem keeping to this schedule.

18. Job safety for both the customer and our workers is your responsibility. Wear hard hats, goggles, steel-toed work shoes where necessary. Be sure that job conditions encourage safety. Monitor both company and individual equipment for proper safety features and safe electrical cords, and inform the production manager of any unsafe conditions.

The Lead Carpenter System

The phrase "lead carpenter system" is bandied about, supported or criticized without much agreement as to what the term really means. There are four steps involved in having a true Lead Carpenter System.

Step One: Assign a carpenter to each job and keep them as a working foreman on that job. This consistency allows the carpenter to learn the entire scope of the job—not just what they're going to do for the next 8 hours. The carpenter has "ownership" of the job and accountability for all the craftsmanship in it. The carpenter develops a good working relationship with the client.

This matching of a lead carpenter to each job will improve your scheduling discipline. You can't begin new jobs until you have an available lead and you can't pull and reassign people to keep more jobs going than you have personnel available to do.

Step Two: Increase the level of the lead carpenter's responsibility. Earlier we outlined how this is a key management level for your company aimed at getting work done right the first time and freeing up your production manager from everyday supervision.

Step Three: Use a one-person base crew. That one person is the lead carpenter.

Most remodeling crews in full-line firms are composed of one, two, or three field employees. At different job stages, all of these variations make economic sense. However, too often companies decide on a basic crew size and do not change as the work requirements change. Often this situation means too many rather than too few people working on a job, and the company loses profit.

The three-person crew with one or two carpenters and one or two helpers is the least frequently seen in residential remodeling. Most remodelers consider it highly inefficient for day-to-day operations and believe that a three-person crew should be used only when it is clearly justified by the nature of the work being done.

The two-person crew—a carpenter and helper—is the most common residential remodeling crew size. If the work calls for two or more people, they should be used. However, remodelers sometimes forget to question whether one or two people are really needed. Any company using this size crew should question the need constantly and separate the two workers whenever possible.

The one-person (lead carpenter) base crew is a definite trend in the industry. While it is still used by a minority of companies, this system appears to produce output (in sales volume) per field worker of $175,000-$250,000 annually. This compares to an $85,000-$100,000 output per person in a two person crew in a traditional carpentry format. In this system, the lead carpenter stays on the job— as long as there is carpentry work—from start to finish and paces the work accordingly.

During phases needing two or more workers, the lead carpenter must call the office to schedule the help he/she needs. During mechanical rough-in and drywall, the lead carpenter often will work on the exterior finish which allows him/her to remain on the job supervising the subs.

SIX BENEFITS OF THE LEAD CARPENTER SYSTEM

O One accountable, responsible person is on the job to provide supervision and quality control. Therefore, less work needs to be redone.

O Between base salary and bonuses, this carpenter can now be paid more highly than the traditional carpenter, so outstanding people can be hired and retained.

O On many additions, using one carpenter spreads out the work so that that person can stay on the job throughout production, and the overall work schedule is not delayed. This practice improves overall job quality and results in fewer errors.

O Field employee productivity improves. Many companies using this system have carpenters producing and supervising work totaling $175,000 to $250,000 in gross sales volume per year.

○ Companies using this system often use subcontractors for every possible function—insulation, siding, roofing, drywall, ceramic, and others. This practice increases the fixed prices in the bid and lessens the risk of a labor overrun. It reduces the number of workers needing direct supervision. Any unexpected contingencies would be negotiated with the subcontractors.

○ With reduced personnel and a more competent and accountable lead carpenter, production managers can often manage $1 to $1.5 million in annual sales volume.

Step Four: Develop a job-cost-based incentive program for the lead carpenter.

Along with giving lead carpenters increased responsibility, many remodelers are using financial incentives to reward outstanding performance. These incentives include bonuses based on meeting or beating the schedule, sharing labor costs that were saved over those estimated, or simply a bonus when a good job has been done.

The most common incentive is based on providing your estimated job costs to the lead who then manages and monitors the actual costs to meet or beat the estimated costs. All labor savings (since this is the most volatile and difficult to control segment) are shared with the lead. There are many variables to consider when determining who receives what part of the incentive.

🖝 COACHING TIP

When you present an incentive program, be sure to call it a trial. Be clear that it will take up to a year to get it running smoothly. Don't make big promises. After all, your personnel have nothing to lose — any bonus is more than they are getting today. Then work like the devil to give out bonuses. Many of your leads won't believe you until it starts to happen. But there is usually at least one carpenter at the beginning who will make it happen on his/her job.

Giving the lead carpenter an incentive to improve job performance has produced considerable production cost improvements in many companies. In addition, an incentive provides you with an objective way to reward high achievers. In many companies, the extra income provided by incentives allows the best carpenters to earn an additional $3,000 to $7,000 a year.

This step is the most difficult to implement in the lead carpenter system, yet it powers the lead carpenter program. If you have a production manager, be sure to share the company's earnings with him/her so they are also tied into helping your leads bring their jobs in on budget.

Carpenter's Helper

The carpenter helper or trainee is an all-purpose worker in many remodeling companies. Often this helper or trainee is learning and working to become a full carpenter. A company may have helpers who run the range from the rank beginner to almost-carpenters. Many a small job has been well run with pride by a skilled carpenter's helper.

The successful remodeler hires these workers with care. Why not invest in tomorrow's outstanding carpenter instead of someone only interested in earning enough money to get to the next weekend? The employee hired can use this position to train for advancement. Many of today's excellent carpenters have advanced from helper or trainee. A local college or university with construction classes may be a source of eager, bright beginners looking for a chance to learn the business. Don't waste this position on a loser.

The Truck Driver

This is a position you do not want to fill if you can avoid it. You definitely do not want a truck driver on the payroll unless your volume is over $1 million. Your field employees, instead of being increasingly efficient, will use this expensive individual and truck as a "go-fer" for materials that should have been ordered for supplier delivery.

However, large volume companies often find they need at least a part time driver and truck for picking up material and hauling trash. Salary for this position is usually low, and because of that, companies often get into the habit of expecting (and receiving) poor performance and high turnover.

No small company can afford even one marginal employee. It's worth paying $2 an hour more for a bright, eager worker who can save the company a great deal of money by handling material carefully, tracking equipment properly, substituting materials accurately, and thinking on his or her feet. Settling for a marginal, "just passing through" person who is a poor worker will ultimately cost more.

Adding a Production Manager

When a remodeler is new and gross sales volume is under $600,000 to $650,000, the owner often fills the three major roles:
salesperson,
administrator, and
production manager

As the company grows larger, you find you must give up day-to-day managing of two of those functions. Usually the first staff person you hire is an office manager. Then you have to decide whether to concentrate your energy in sales or production. The other function is delegated to a new employee. When deciding which function to retain, remember that choosing to retain production as your primary responsibility will mean that—

☞ A large number of the company's employees will report directly to you.

☞ Production needs will take precedence over all other types of work, and production is fraught with crises that must be handled within a short period of time.

☞ Production work is never done. More work is always waiting.

For that reason, it is usually wiser to hire the production manager and retain the sales function. Don't make the mistake many owners make. They continue to handle production to the overload stage and then expect to hire an outside person, saddle that person with the work overload, and expect him/her to succeed. Needless to say, that practice does not work.

In addition, you may have been handling the work helter-skelter, and now you expect the new production manager to set up systems and paperwork. If remodelers avoid overloading new employees when transferring their production duties, the new systems and paperwork that are so desperately needed will be learned and accomplished more quickly. And the business will function better.

🔔 COACHING TIP

Some think that if you upgrade the traditional carpenter to today's lead carpenter, you can delete the position of production manager. That has not been our experience. Certainly, you do transfer some of the duties of the production manager to the lead carpenter but there is still a role for someone who coordinates all the various jobs and resources, hires and coaches field employees, does special order purchasing, etc. So whether you, the owner, handle the function or whether you hire a separate production manager, someone's got to do the job.

The Production Manager

The title *production manager* clearly stresses the management function. Production managers rarely fail because they don't understand the technical side of remodeling. They fail because they have few skills for managing people or because their management and organizational skills are weak.

While the production manager certainly plays a technical-watchdog role in guarding the company against poor construction, he/she is most importantly a manager of people. Production managers need excellent sales, negotiating, and educational skills to work with clients on a day-to-day basis. To succeed in helping production personnel progress through their companies, they must be coaches, trainers, and motivators. They also must be able to convey the field worker's viewpoint—positive or negative—to you.

The production manager is responsible for the entire production department of the company. He/she coordinates all activities related to the actual remodeling and renovation of jobs sold by the sales department, and takes a job from inception to final completion. The production department coordinates all the labor, materials, and subcontractors of the company. This responsibility includes maintaining customer satisfaction through the job.

Production Manager's Job Description

General Description: *The production manager has primary responsibility for seeing that each project meets these three goals:*

1. Job costs come in at or under the estimated budget

2. The job is completed on time

3. The client is left highly satisfied and likely to refer others to us for remodeling.

If our company has trouble meeting these goals, the production manager is an important part of the team that finds solutions that enable the company to meet these three critical goals on all future projects.

The production manager directs all field employees, subcontractors, material suppliers, inspectors, and others in the efforts needed to achieve these goals. This includes hiring, firing, training and coaching field employees, as well as organizing and scheduling the work.

REGULAR DUTIES:

Preconstruction -
- Reviews final plans and specifications to ensure that no problems will arise in filing for and obtaining building permits.

➤ Field checks each job sold and turned in by the sales department and checks the salesperson's cost breakdown to determine whether the job can be done to the company's established quality level at the specified profit.

➤ Sets up jobs accepted by the company as ready for construction. Orders all special order material and tracks delivery times assuring that material arrives at the job when needed.

➤ Negotiates prices with subcontractors. Writes work orders, and maintains specifications/requisition records of these activities for each job.

➤ Meets with the salesperson and the customers in a preconstruction conference to discuss scope, potential problems, and decisions made by the customers.

Throughout Construction -

➤ Maintains frequent (at least once a week) communication with the customer throughout the job in person (while checking the job), by phone, or in writing.

➤ Oversees the prompt triggering and pickup of all draws by the lead carpenter.

➤ Takes responsibility for all routine change orders. Makes sure those orders carry fixed prices. When change orders involve substantial work, the production manager coordinates with the sales department on the pricing and selling of these.

➤ Conducts a precompletion walk-through with the customer and the lead carpenter to prepare a quality control punchlist. Expedites the completion of the punchlist and follows up until the final payment check is collected.

➤ Approves all requests for payment to subcontractors. Verifies that they are properly allocated to a job, priced accordingly, and that the invoices reflect actual shipments.

➤ Coordinates all necessary inspections during the course of a job.

Ongoing -

➤ Maintains an adequate work force of carpenters and trainees or helpers to meet the needs of the company. This responsibility includes hiring and training of the labor force and the authority to fire as well.

The production manager holds monthly meetings of all carpenters to keep them informed and discuss and solve any problems.

➤ Reviews job cost reports biweekly for all jobs and checks whether actual costs exceed estimated costs in any area. When there are cost overruns, researches where and why and puts an action plan in place to avoid such overruns on future jobs. The production manager is responsible for creating a plan with the lead carpenter on how future money will be saved on the job that is overrunning.

➤ Maintains all vehicles, tools, and equipment in excellent operating condition through regularly scheduled maintenance and prompt repairs when necessary.

➤ Submits to management a monthly production report including progress on each job, percentage of completion, estimated total dollar volume for each job, and an estimated gross profit on each job.

➤ Devises incentive programs for individual crew members to maximize performance.

➤ Performs other duties as assigned.

Education, Experience, and Skills Needed

- High school diploma and some college or equivalent experience and/or training preferred

- Basic knowledge of remodeling and construction trades, practices, procedures, techniques, equipment, materials, specifications, estimating, quality control, cost control, safety, and applicable building codes and zoning ordinances

- Supervisory experience

- Strong communication skills

- Basic mathematics skills

Whether you, the company owner, are the production manager or you hire a production manager, these varied tasks need to be done in order to keep production efficient and effective. Aim to develop a smoothly functioning production team and a set of systems that will expand with a minimum of turmoil as the company grows.

The Production Assistant

If the production manager (whether it's you or an employee) becomes swamped by work, an inexpensive solution is to develop a production assistant position. Having a production assistant should allow the production manager to handle approximately $500,000 in additional volume. A well-trained assistant can also provide invaluable help to the salespeople in pricing.

Much production work must be done over the phone in an office setting. This work includes pricing, ordering, subcontracting, scheduling, and maintaining frequent contact with clients. An office-based production assistant can handle many of these duties while backing up the production manager in his/her duties.

In choosing a production assistant, the production manager should look for a bright, enthusiastic clerical person who is ready for a challenge.

The person selected for the production assistant position needs to handle details extremely well, be a list-maker and a schedule-watcher. With excellent, detailed, on-the-job training, the production assistant often becomes indispensable to the company.

Production Assistant Job Description

The production assistant assists the production manager in the accomplishment of a construction job. The production manager is the production assistant's direct supervisor and assigns exact duties to the production assistant.

Specific Duties:
Prepare a job site file for the lead carpenter to use. This file should contain:
   a. Permit and set of plans
   b. Most recent set of construction plans
   c. Specifications of contract with prices blanked out
   d. Copies of change orders
   e. Cut sheets of appliances, special heaters, etc.
   f. Rough-in information for windows, skylights, doors, if actual items are not yet on site
   g. Work flow chart or schedule

2. Prepare production manager's job file for office use, with sections for:
   a. Plans
   b. Contract
   c. Change orders
   d. Billing invoices, copies of payments
   e. Lists of ordered materials
   f. Lists of materials still to be ordered
   g. Subcontractor contracts
   h. Copy of permit
   i. Estimator cost sheets
   j. Flow chart or schedule

3. Update these files regularly with all pertinent changes and paperwork as needed.

4. Assist production manager in materials ordering. All orders must be okayed by production manager, and should include date ordered, date expected, delivery instructions, and cost with tax and delivery. Keep calendar with due dates for various special orders and telephone to confirm actual delivery as the due dates approach. Send out written confirmation on critical components.

5. Check billings against order prices and estimator's cost sheets. Point out any discrepancy to production manager.

6. Process and file subcontractor yearly agreement forms, copies of licenses, certificates of insurance, and individual job subcontracts as received.

7. Be sure all subcontractors receive updated plans whenever these are revised, and that they are kept aware of any change order items relevant to them.

8. Type change orders as generated by production manager, file, and prepare invoice for collection. Update expected job costs with change order estimate of materials, labor and subs cost.

9. Receive calls from carpenters, owners, and subs when production manager is not available, and take appropriate action.

10. Assist production manager in assembling monthly job cost and production reports.

11. Prepare and send out customer evaluation surveys one month after construction is complete. Monitor return of surveys, route to appropriate personnel who worked on a project, and file for possible future marketing use.

12. Set up and maintain completed job files to be kept available for reference for at least five years after construction completion.

13. Log all warranty calls, and file in job files after completion.

Production Meetings

Keeping production up-to-speed and on target will involve two types of meetings in most companies. There will be a weekly in-office production meeting and a second, monthly, field meeting.

The weekly in-office production meeting would include you and the production manager. It normally would be scheduled for 60 to 90 minutes. This meeting gives you a "window" into production and encourages the production manager to focus on the three key production goals.

The Production Manager reports on:

☞ dollar volume of work of what type in backlog

☞ dollar volume of work currently in production

☞ current monthly production output

☞ any budget or scheduling problems

☞ any personnel shortages or problems

☞ subs and supplier issues

Job cost reports would be reviewed regularly as well as the individual schedules for each job. Any customer dissatisfaction problems are reviewed and strategies for handling discussed.

If your company is large enough to have field personnel other than yourself, it's big enough to have *monthly field meetings*—even if they are held on the tailgate of the pickup. These meetings allow you to train everyone at once, to disseminate important information to everyone and to keep your finger on the pulse of the field.

COACHING TIP

Be sure to follow these tried-and-true guidelines for successful meetings:

1. Always start and stop the meeting at the announced time.

2. Have an agenda with expected times listed next to each item (for example, *3. New Osha rules—15 minutes*) so you can keep the meeting on track.

3. Have a facilitator who will move items along, quiet the overly talkative and encourage the shy.

4. When addressing a problem or proposed change, always write down the steps to be taken, the person who will handle and the time by which they will report back. Update this list each meeting.

Subcontractors and Suppliers

In-house carpenters and helpers are only part of the production team. The subcontractor portion of job costs often equals the labor portion. Indeed, material purchases may also equal dollar volume for the labor on a given job. If a job is to go well and if a remodeler is to thrive, both subcontractors and suppliers must be part of the team.

Subcontractors as Team Members

Many remodelers simply shop price to find the "best" subcontractor. Every job is fully bid out. Any given subcontractor may do a few jobs and then begin to lose out to a lower-priced sub. Some subs may even offer low prices initially to get work and raise them later when the remodeler is used to working with them.

Today, the method of choosing subs on the basis of price alone is losing ground to an awareness that outstanding subs, like good remodelers, are never the cheapest. The well-run remodeling business needs subcontracting companies that are also well-run.

Finding great subs requires searching for good candidates, making sure their prices represent good value, and then teaming up with them. As with employees, there is always an initial orientation period while a sub learns how your company operates. If you have chosen well, you may be using the same electrician, plumber, or other sub for 5, 10, or 15 years.

This search for long term alliances must be balanced with keeping value-based pricing. Using two subs in each specialty often helps to keep their pricing pencil sharpened and their customer service topnotch on your behalf. Don't let subs get too comfortable by ruling out all competition.

Constant turnover in subcontractors is as disruptive to the remodeler as constant turnover in employees. The consumer views everyone on the job as part of the remodeler's team and responsibility. Thus, subcontractors must be as well-qualified, industrious, personable, and conscientious as the remodeler's own personnel.

Outstanding subcontractors can pick the remodelers for whom they want to work. To keep excellent subs a remodeler must provide a profitable and efficient working environment for them.

Subcontracting Carpentry

While this chapter started by focusing on employed carpenters, there has been a minor trend in the last few years of remodelers moving to carpentry subs. That allows the remodeler to have maximum freedom and flexibility in the marketplace. Quality does not have to suffer, especially if you are willing to devote as much attention to bringing your sub into line with company policies as you would with an employee.

When carpentry subs are used on a job, the production manager must spend extra time and effort networking all the various trades and supervising the job more fully than when there is a lead carpenter acting on the company's behalf. The carpentry sub is focused only on their own trade and cannot be expected to supervise the plumber's rough-in or help the electrician.

Avoiding Captive Subs

In the past many remodelers have treated employees—salespeople, carpenters, and installers—as subcontractors even though they worked directly for the remodelers. This practice relieved the remodeler of collecting withholding taxes, paying the employer's Social Security contribution, Workers' Compensation insurance, federal and state unemployment insurance, and other such levies. You often pay a 25 to 30 percent labor burden on an employee that is not required for a subcontractor.

However, the Federal Government wants true employees treated as such, and it investigates companies to be sure that those claimed as subcontractors are truly independent businesses. When a subcontractor is actually functioning as an employee, he/she is called a "captive" subcontractor. The Internal Revenue Service of the Federal Government can and will levy stiff penalties as well as back taxes and premiums on the business for using captive subs.

Since the IRS rules are under review and are subject to change, you'll want to discuss the captive sub issue with an attorney if your company operates in a gray area.

Ground Rules for Subs

If subcontractors are going to be part of the team, they need to know what game is being played and just what the rules are. Just as a policy manual simplifies employee training and is an agreement between employer and employee, so a remodeler should negotiate a new written agreement with each subcontractor on a yearly basis.

This agreement should cover all issues the remodeler believes are pertinent. It should spell out any areas in which disagreements could arise. These might include whether or not site visits are required of the subcontractor before a price is submitted, and who will pay for trash removal—including debris from demolition, boxes from fittings and fixtures, and other trash. The agreement should tell how invoices are to be submitted and what procedure you will use to pay them. It should also answer such questions as whether the sub can do work on the side for the customer.

ANNUAL SUBCONTRACTOR AGREEMENT

Company Name: _____ Specialty: _____

Address:_____

Business Phone: _____ Emergency Phone: _____

Licensed In: _____ Lic.Rec'd:_____ Ins.Cert.Rec'd:_____

We at XYZ CONSTRUCTION welcome your association with our company. This agreement lists our subcontracting policies. Please sign at the bottom to signify that you agree to abide by these policies. We look forward to a pleasant and profitable business relationship with your company.

---

1. As a subcontractor for our company, you have become part of our team. We look to you to help 'debug' our jobs. If you anticipate a problem not addressed in our plans, or find any code violation or technical problem, please notify us promptly.

All bids should be based on a job site visit. If you prefer not to make such a visit, any later problem caused by conflicting conditions becomes your problem and your responsibility.

2. All your personnel on our job should support our company and speak well of it. You are an integral part of our marketing program. Both our businesses stand to lose or gain by our job behavior. What a difference there is between the mechanic who says to the customer, "Boy, this contractor always messes me up. He's never ready when he says he'll be. All he cares about is how fast I can go," and the mechanic who says, "It's always a pleasure working for this company. They give me a chance to do my best work."

3. REFERRALS: Over the course of our work together, we will refer appropriate work to you, and look to you to supply us with leads as well. If any of our customers request work directly from you within one year of your work for us on that job, you will need our permission to work directly with our customer.

4. CHANGES: All changes must be approved by our superintendent or our office. If time is a problem, you may proceed with our verbal approval, but we ask you to follow up with a written change order. No prices may be given directly to the customer.

5. LICENSE AND INSURANCE: Please send us a copy of your license and an insurance certificate showing Workers Compensation and liability and auto/truck coverage. We must have this in our files before we issue any draws.

6. JOB SCHEDULE: If, for any reason, you get to a job and additional work is needed before you can proceed, please call our office immediately. We can often solve your problem without delay. If we can't, we will work to solve the immediate problem and to avoid such work stoppages in the future.

7. TRASH: Your work area is to be left broom clean by you at the end of each day. Sweepings may be left neatly on our designated trash pile. Unless prior arrangements have been made, any other trash is to be hauled by you on at least a weekly basis.

We stock dust protection materials on the job. Your mechanics must dust protect any unprotected area they are working in, before starting work.

8. MATERIALS: Acceptance and unloading of deliveries of your materials, their storage and protection, insurance, and all other risk of loss of your materials or equipment is your responsibility. Any items you remove from the job to be held for safekeeping are your responsibility to store and protect (i.e., thermostats, light fixtures, plumbing fixtures, etc.).

9. WARRANTY: All labor and material is to be fully guaranteed by you for one year after substantial completion. Any manufacturer's warranties that exceed this one-year period are to be given to the customers for their use.

10. CONTRACTS: We work by written contract. This contract should include the date of plans and specifications. We assume your subcontract includes all work listed and shown unless otherwise specified, including labor, material, and necessary equipment.

11. DRAWS: We do not pay any "upon signing" draws. Please tie your draws to rough-in and final, including any required inspections (i.e., "upon plumbing rough-in and inspection"). The final draw should include both final inspection and customer approval.

Subcontractor_____ Date _____

Keeping Outstanding Subcontractors

Finding, learning to work with, and keeping outstanding subcontractors is a long term investment. Here are five guidelines that will cement your long term relationship with your present subcontractors and allow you to attract a constant stream of new and talented subs:

◄ Pay promptly. Honor payment promises whether the customer has paid you or not.

◄ Schedule accurately and keep subcontractors aware of schedule changes.

◄ Meet on a monthly basis with the company's most important subcontractors.

◄ Ask advice from subcontractors on how to improve the relationship and the remodeling company's operations to make jobs more efficient and profitable.

◄ Treat them as part of the team; share your dollar volume goals and discuss what portion of that volume can be theirs if they "team up" with you.

To a subcontractor, the two most important items on this list are quick payment and reliability in scheduling. Be scrupulous in honoring payment promises whether or not the customer has paid the remodeler. Inaccurate scheduling that requires a subcontractor to make repeated trips to a job only to find it is not yet ready will send the sub looking for other work quickly.

Consider having private monthly meetings with all major subcontractors. You might just stop to have a cup of coffee together to talk about what is going well and any areas that have hit snags.

Selecting Your Supplier Team

Reliable suppliers who care are an important part of your team. You have many concerns related to the quality of the materials they supply, the extra value the individual supplier adds to the transaction and their willingness to be a team member who is sometimes asked to go an extra mile. Here are 20 questions that will help you separate the high value supplier from the low value product-mover:

? Do they provide good quality materials?

? Do they stock the desired product locally?

? Do they deliver to the jobsite and do it when they promise they will? Will they stack materials inside, or do they provide only curbside delivery?

? Do they extend the credit terms the remodeler may need?

? Do they provide a discount to the professional remodeler? Do they provide even deeper discounts after a company's purchases total a particular amount, so a company can monitor its sales to achieve the better discount?

? If a remodeler is incorporated, will the suppliers accept signing of their credit agreements under the aegis of the corporation or does the remodeler (and perhaps the spouse) have to sign personally?

? Will the suppliers help do a ballpark estimate of materials for a large job? Needless to say, final estimates should be based on the remodeler's own careful calculations.

? Will they occasionally work out special delivery requests?

? Will they help locate hard-to-find materials?

? Do they stock and willingly provide the manufacturers' sales literature for use in selling their products?

? Do they provide cooperative advertising dollars if a remodeler uses a product in quantity?

? Are they willing to stock a product for a remodeler if he/she uses it in quantity?

? Will they agree to hold their prices valid for a time period?

? Are they set up to accept orders over a fax system to save time and decrease errors?

? Do they use computerized billing rather than handwritten and hand-priced invoices which can be confusing, hard to read, and more error prone?

? Do they have special cutting or milling abilities that the remodeler may need?

? Do they have a showroom or display that will be useful in showing customers the product? If so, are they careful to discuss only list prices with the consumers?

? What do they charge for restocking materials that are returned?

? Do they readily replace defective materials?

? Will they band lumber to make pilferage and theft more difficult?

Your well-chosen suppliers will either help you look like a hero on the job when all the correct supplies arrive at the right time or a dimwit when the wrong materials arrive at the wrong time. Be sure you've got supplier superstars on your team.

Your Production All Stars

Sales makes promises, production delivers on them. You are only as good as your delivery team. Think of the impact on your company if you insist that each team slot —

your suppliers,

your subs,

your carpenters,

your carpenter helpers and laborers,

your truck driver,

and your production manager—

is filled by an all star player. Then give them the training and coaching and the procedures that let them shine (next chapter) and you'll leave your best competition in the dust!

14

■ ■

Delivering the Completed Job

Remodeling jobs involve so many people, products, and details that they cannot be produced well without considerable organization. The trend in recent years in the remodeling industry is to create checks and balances within the production department to reduce errors and avoid redoing work, to create customer satisfaction, and focus employees' attention on the job's cost and schedule.

The goals of most production procedures are to—

○ Debug the job up front

○ Move the job smoothly out of sales and into production

○ Increase profitability and customer satisfaction

Organize production well and you'll—

○ Save time. Five minutes spent to solve a problem before a job starts will save you 30 or more minutes if it arises during the job.

○ Save money. Problems found early can be efficiently handled without causing construction delays. The solution can be built in at the appropriate time. Otherwise the company does it wrong the first time, has to redo the work, and loses money and customer confidence.

O Reduce work to be redone and present a rational, standardized approach to common problems so employees do not constantly need to think up solutions to routine problems.

O Help employees do their jobs better and more efficiently. Systems provide a structure in which the employee can flourish. They are particularly helpful for new employees.

O Make customer satisfaction more predictable and easier to achieve.

O Reveal any situations in which there are gaps in responsibility or overlapping duties.

Effective Production Systems

Successful remodelers generally agree on the production steps needed for a company to deliver well. These include:

Pre-construction–

—◀ Transfer of the job from sales

—◀ Establishing job files

—◀ Holding a site walk-through

—◀ Holding a preconstruction conference with the customer

—◀ Scheduling job progress

—◀ Contracting with subs

—◀ Ordering special or custom materials

During construction–

—◀ Scheduling the production staff

—◀ Issuing and controlling change orders

—◀ Collecting draws on time

—◀ Checking quality control at close-in

◄ Inspecting the job before punchlist

◄ Completing the final walkthrough with the customer

After construction–

◄ Handling warranty callbacks

If your company is small and you, the owner, are the salesperson, production manager and carpenter, you have a much more simplified list of procedures. Note that over half of these steps happen before construction begins. In many ways, the preproduction systems are the most productive and profitable in terms of debugging and developing strategy for a job.

The Handoff from Sales

This handoff is one of the trickiest and most trouble-plagued areas in production. In small companies there is one handoff from owner/salesperson to lead carpenter. In large companies there is likely to be a second handoff from the salesperson to the production manager. Often the salesperson wants to move on to other potential sales and simply gathers up all the assorted materials associated with the new contract and dumps them on the production manager's desk or hands them off to the lead carpenter. While one of the most important goals of the first few steps in these procedures is to free the salesperson to go back to selling, he/she must package the job properly and participate in the full communication of vital information to help assure production success. In most remodeling companies, the salesperson is responsible for delivering the following items in the file they turn over to production:

☞ Two copies of the signed contract

☞ Two sets of signed plans

☞ Any detailed specification sheets

☞ The check for the signing draw or a receipt for it

⭘ Financing papers

⭘ The estimate with a clear and concise summary on a cover sheet including the subcontractor bids, materials lists with prices, and the source of the prices

⭘ Clear copies of all orders for materials. (For example: for a kitchen job, the company may require the salesperson to order cabinets and include a copy of the completed order in this contract package.)

⭘ A copy of the building permit if the salesperson is responsible for obtaining it

⭘ A key to the building in which the job is to be done

Some companies have a checklist to make this transfer easy. Usually it spells out who is to do what in the handoff. Examine the important details of this transfer in your company and sort them as to which steps you want to be standard.

Handoff Checklist

Here is a sample of the type of checklist that is often used by remodelers to systematize the handoff between the salesperson and the production staff.

Customer:_____   Contract Date: _____

Salesperson:_____   Start Date:_____

RECEIVED FROM
SALES DEPARTMENT

☐ Two sets signed plans

☐ Two sets signed contract

☐ Signed right of rescission form

☐ 'Before' photographs

☐ Signed draw check or receipt

☐ Subcontractor bids:

    ☐ Electrical

    ☐ Plumbing

    ☐ HVAC

    ☐ Masonry

    ☐ Other

☐ Financing papers in order

☐ Materials list, accurately priced
with source and date

☐ Cabinet order sent;
copy on file

☐ All open items priced and
closed

☐ Change order signed

☐ Plat ordered

☐ Customer thank-you from
salesperson

PRODUCTION CHECKLIST BEFORE
JOB START

☐ Plans reviewed and accepted

☐ Bids reviewed and accepted

☐ Job site walk-through complete

☐ Job measurements checked

☐ Cabinet measurements
reviewed, checked against
order

☐ Start and completion dates OK

☐ Permit:

    ☐ Application complete

    ☐ Check from bookkeeping

    ☐ Permit received

☐ Flow chart prepared

☐ Schedule board set up

☐ Pre-construction conference
with owner complete

☐ Phone on job

☐ Key received

☐ Underground utility check OK

Acceptance from sales by:

_____

Prod. Manager_____   Date_____

Establishing Job Files

The contract package received from sales is copied and distributed among the various individuals who need the information. Otherwise, each person—the bookkeeper, the carpenter, the production manager—asks independently for what they need. This is inefficient and time consuming. Here are some of the files that may be needed in your company:

The Legal File. Be sure to safely store a copy of the signed contract, a set of the plans, and specifications. This file on legal matters should be separate from files used daily because any file in daily use runs the risk of having papers removed and possibly lost.

The Working Office File. Usually the production manager is responsible for this file. It contains the contract, plans, specifications, orders, confirmations, contracts with subcontractors, production schedule, customer records, change orders, and notes.

The Field File. This file is created for the lead carpenter's use. It includes plans, specifications, details from the contract, copies of change orders, production schedule, telephone numbers of subcontractors and suppliers.

The Bookkeepers File. Often the bookkeeper receives a copy of the contract or a list of contract draws, the total contract amount, and notices of contracts with subcontractors and the amounts, a detailed estimate of labor and materials by task for use in producing job costs, change orders, purchase orders, and any other financial commitments related to the jobs.

Save yourself time and money by establishing the files you need all at the same time.

Holding a Site Walk-Through

If your company is large enough that the salesperson and the production manager are two different people, they should arrange a site walk-through. The lead carpenter who will be working on the job should also be a participant. Try to meet without the client so that questions—and answers—can be frank and open. Before meeting, all parties should study the job plans and specifications and write down their questions.

During this walk-through the salesperson can educate the production manager on the job specifications at the site. It's a chance for the production manager and lead carpenter to discuss unanticipated problems. An effective walk-through of a moderate-size job is likely to take 60 to 90 minutes. It should include the strategy of the job as well as the actual construction details. Some of the strategy questions to be answered include—

How will the surrounding household areas be protected?

Where will materials be stored?

Will a bathroom and phone in the building be designated for field use? If not, will a phone be installed and if so, where? Where will a portable toilet be placed?

The Preconstruction Conference

The client joins the above group for the Preconstruction Conference so it can be handy to schedule them on the same day. Again, this conference is most productive if it includes the salesperson, the production manager, and the lead carpenter as well as the customer. This conference has four objectives:

O To introduce the customer to the production manager and the lead carpenter

O To make clear to the customer that the production department is taking charge of the job and that the salesperson is stepping aside. In fact, the production manager should lead this meeting.

○ Preview exactly what is going to be constructed and what is not included. This addresses any discrepancies in the customer's understanding of the planned job.

○ To let the customer know how to work with production and what will be expected of each party.

The production manager reviews the plans and contract specifications in great detail with the customer. If any selections are open or change orders pending, they are handled at this conference, or the customer is given a deadline for handling them.

Many potential problems surface at these Preconstruction Conferences. The production department can take care of them before construction begins—causing the least disruption in the job. Often customers have discussed many options during the design and bidding process, and they may believe that some items are included that really are not. It's better to find out about them at this stage—when changes can still be made —than to have an angry, disappointed customer later.

Scheduling Job Progress

The production manager, lead carpenter, and the salesperson now return to the office to schedule the job they have explored in detail during the site walk-through and the preconstruction conference. See the previous chapter for greater detail on types and uses of schedules.

Subcontracting

Once the production manager is highly familiar with the new job, it's time to contract with the subcontractors figured into the estimate or—at least occasionally—to get another price in each specialty.

To prevent problems, the production manager uses written subcontractor contracts that include as much detail as possible. These contracts need to be tied into the plans and specifications and include the total dollar amount as well as the draw schedule. Contracts should be clear in specifying who is supplying the materials to be used and installed by the subcontractors.

Ordering Special Materials

Most remodeling jobs require some materials that must be special ordered. These can be ordered by phone, by mail, or by fax and are usually handled by the production manager. Orders that are phoned in should be followed up with a written confirmation specifying the item(s), quantity, brand, grade, type, price (including tax and delivery), delivery address, and the promised delivery time.

COACHING TIP

Faxes have made material pricing simpler than ever before. Simply write up a request for pricing with the list of materials. Don't put any supplier name on the base sheet. Then fax to 2 or 3 suppliers and await their return faxes.

Promised delivery dates should be noted on a calendar. Also jot down a reminder to call and check on up-coming deliveries one week before the delivery date. A delay in the delivery of special orders can seriously harm a job schedule.

The production manager or the lead carpenter makes careful lists of all the materials that will be needed during the first few weeks of the job. These are ordered for delivery to the site as well. Many remodeling companies handle ordering of the major lumber loads from the office while day-to-day lumber needs are called in from the job.

And Now The Job Begins

As is evident in the long list of procedures the production manager oversees, the company will be more efficient and productive if you aggressively pursue a clean transfer between sales and production, and a clear agreement with the customer as to what will be constructed. By developing an organized approach to the production of the job that emphasizes careful groundwork you are already saving money and time and the job is only about to begin.

Weekly Production Schedule

Create a system to chart all your jobs and production personnel for the week. Many companies schedule subcontractors as well as in-house personnel for the following week. Your weekly production schedule should include major material deliveries, inspections, draws, and any outstanding items to be handled.

WEEKLY PRODUCTION SCHEDULE

WEEK OF Jan. 25

JOB NAME	MONDAY	TUESDAY	WEDNESDAY	THURSDAY	FRIDAY	NOTES
Muldoon	Joe / Terry	footing insp. / mason in p.m.	Mason	Stan Terry	Stan Terry	get dry-wall prices
Smith	plbg. r. Jn a.m. elec. r. Jn pm	mech. inspection close in inspection	Insulation a.m. Stock Drywall	Drywall →		order hdw. keyed to owners pre. slct set
Aaron	Stan	Stan Joe	Stan Joe	HVAC Elec Plumbing	Mech. Insp. Closein Insp.	set up ceram. tile pick up countertop
Jones	Dave Terry	Dave Terry	Dave Terry	Dave Roofer	Dave Roofer	schedule mechanical
Packer	Job Walk-thru Preconstr Conf.	—	—	—	Job Start Demo Homeshell	order out matls. for Monday, Feb. 1
Cramer	complete punchlist collect	—		—	—	—

Producing a company-wide schedule every week assures that the production manager and staff focus on each job in the context of what is happening in the entire company. Thus, if the same plumber is scheduled for two different jobs at the same time, that mistake will be caught and corrected before it causes a problem. This schedule allows anyone in the company to help customers who call in to see what will occur on their jobs during the week or families of field personnel who need to get in touch with them.

Once the weekly schedule is completed, the subs can be called with their schedule for the week and material deliveries can be set up.

VOICES OF EXPERIENCE...

Mark Goldsborough, president of MITCHELL, BEST & GOLDS-BOROUGH, INC., Rockville, MD, has designed a job log book to be used on each of his jobs. There's a page for each day's notes and spaces to record the weather, any inspections, sub visits and homeowner requests. Carpenters use the book to keep tabs on job labor, record emergency phone numbers, track owner draws and refer to time card task codes. One copy of the daily log stays bound in the book and one copy goes weekly to Goldsborough who says "The log has proved invaluable in creating an accurate job diary that we refer to again and again."

Controlling Change Orders

Change orders seem to be a necessary evil. They often add volume to the job but can be difficult to mark up adequately since individual prices are so visible to the client. And change orders interrupt the pace of a job and extend its completion date. Changes may become so rampant on a job that you lose control of the job, the budget and the schedule. And the customer always blames you!

COACHING TIP

Change orders often total an additional 3-5% of the remodeling job. Many remodelers get sloppy about charging for changes that cost them more to execute. But can you afford to lose that 3-5% from your bottom line? We don't know any remodeler who can.

Emphasize to the client throughout the sales process that you want to avoid change orders. This pushes the customer to make decisions, and it pushes you to close every open item, every selection, every possible change. Set up ground rules for change orders:

- They must be written and signed by the homeowner before the work begins.
- They are to be paid 100 percent upon signing.
- They carry a $25 to $50 administrative fee.
- The change order form carries the message "Change orders extend completion date."
- Change orders should be contracted at a fixed price whenever possible, rather than on a time-and-materials

basis. Working on a time-and-materials basis creates a tough tracking burden on the carpenter and the production manager. It also can produce some unhappy surprises for the consumer when the item comes in at a price that is higher than expected.

Change orders should be carefully worded in plain English so that your client knows exactly what they are and are not getting, and so that the carpenters can work accurately from the written descriptions:

Rather than saying "Install new door," say "Install new 2/6 x 6/8 hollow-core, birch-faced door in existing opening between baby's nursery and master bedroom. Door to open back against bookshelf wall in baby's room and be equipped with a brass-finish, round knob [brand and #]. Trim to match the stock, one-piece, clam-shell trim in both bedrooms. Price does not include painting or staining." The latter description makes clear all the work involved, explains important details to the carpenter and supports your pricing.

Managing Materials

Materials in remodeling seem to fall into three major categories:

- special orders,
- large basic lumber and hardware orders, and
- spot material orders.

Special Orders. Special items must be ordered ahead of the other materials because they are not stocked by local suppliers or because they are to be custom made. Often these special materials are expensive, difficult to obtain, and cannot be returned. In ordering materials and supplies, a phone or fax order should be followed up by an order confirmation letter that lists the items, quantities, measurements, grade, type, brand, color, price (including any delivery or freight charges), taxes, and other details, as well as the promised delivery time.

Large Lumber and Hardware Orders. These large, predictable purchases of basic building materials can be ordered in bulk from the local supplier who delivers them to the jobsite. Deliveries are frequently made in stages so that the materials are delivered just before they are needed. This practice avoids crowding the remodeling site and cuts down on possible pilfering or theft if the materials have to be stored outdoors. Again, using a fax saves time and provides a written backup.

Spot Purchases. Sometimes the need to order certain materials cannot be foreseen. Often these orders are for a special item needed to solve an unanticipated problem, small amounts of materials needed to finish up a particular task or to tide the crew over until a delayed delivery arrives. These small orders must be picked up by the company truck driver or by another employee.

☞ COACHING TIP

If you or your production manager are spending any time picking up materials for your field personnel, consider that time totally wasted. You are doing the work of an $8-12 per hour employee. Don't do it.

Spot purchases often involve buying from the closest—but not the most competitive—supplier, and the time to make the pickup could be better spent on other tasks. Each pickup could cost your company as much as $25 in employee time. Multiply a month's worth of pickups by $25 and you'll see how much money you are losing. You don't have a line item in your estimate for this material fetching service. Tremendous vigilance and training of personnel is necessary to keep these orders to a minimum.

 COACHING TIP

Every so often take your supplier tickets and separate out those that were picked up by your personnel rather than delivered by the supplier. Review these tickets to determine if a select few employees are doing more pickups than others. Multiply the number of pickups by your estimate of the cost of the personnel time. You may be shocked. After all, there's no line item in your estimate for spot pickups.

Standardizing Materials

There is a strong move in remodeling toward standardizing the most frequently specified materials. Here are seven benefits:

- A reliable supply, preferably stocked by a local wholesaler, can be purchased in larger quantities.

- Larger purchases mean deeper discounts from the supplier.

- Because you've limited the choices, pricing for estimating will be easier.

- Invoices are easier to check because commonly used prices become familiar to company employees.

- Standard products that can be reliably warranted cut down on callbacks.

- Products can be chosen which are locally unavailable at home centers so that price comparisons are more difficult for the consumer.

○ The number of different products used is reduced so employees can learn the installation process more readily. Therefore, installation becomes more and more efficient.

Because of this increased efficiency in pricing, markup, and installation, standardization improves your profitability and productivity.

Standardizing Construction Systems

Consider standardizing as many construction methods and components as possible. This standardization program can take up to a year to complete, and should be a joint effort by both the sales and the production departments.

For example, if you build decks on a regular basis, you could offer one to three standard deck rails. The sketches can be drawn, priced on a lineal-foot basis, and copied for future use. When a prospect wants an estimate on the cost of a deck, offer the stock railing system, and only build a custom rail design if the customer requests it.

Using a stock rail means the company can price quickly, order quickly, and build quickly and efficiently. The stock rail thus becomes less expensive. Estimating for a custom rail will be slower and less sure because the rail will have to be estimated from scratch, and the carpenter will have to figure out how to construct the custom rail. Thus the custom rail will be considerably more expensive for the consumer.

When big business enters a market such as fast foods, standardization is the byword. Each action and each offering is carefully examined to see how efficiency and economy can be built into the system. If you take this same approach, you can make your company significantly more cost and energy efficient. But be sure to balance this efficiency and economy with aesthetics and individuality.

Collecting Money Effectively

Effective money collection begins with how well you educate the customer during the sales process. When the contract is reviewed and signed, the draws should be explained in detail. At that time, you explain to the customer that the company will phone a few days before the draw is due. Then the customer is to give the check to the lead carpenter or production manager on the appropriate day.

SMART COLLECTING

Improve your collection process with these four strategies:

☞ Draws should be based on the "start of" a phase rather than "completion of." When work starts is quite clear, but deciding when a job is completely finished can produce endless discussion and argument which can delay payment.

☞ For a large job, stipulate many small draws ($10,000 or under). It is easier for the customer to pay smaller amounts more frequently. A few companies have the customer escrow all money for the job at the time the contract is signed to be certain that the money will be available when needed.

☞ Make the last draw dependent on "substantial completion" (defined as the point at which the space is usable for the purpose for which it is built). This solves the potential problem of a customer holding an entire final draw because one cabinet knob is backordered.

☞ A Maryland remodeler makes the next-to-last draw the "substantial completion" draw. His final draw of $500 is made upon "completion of the punchlist." Other remodelers allow the customer to hold back 200 percent of the value of any unfinished punchlist items from the final draw. Thus if the value of the unfinished items is $100, the owner would hold $200 until they were completed.

Clients rarely present a collection problem *during* the job. Getting payment for the final bill is usually the collection problem—if there is one. For that reason no extra charges should be allowed to wait for the final invoice. The customer should pay for any change orders at signing. Any time-and-materials charges and extra charges on selections should be billed and collected before the final bill. Keeping the charges up-to-date requires a lot of effort and energy for a small company, but it is a critical ingredient in effective money collection.

Checking Quality Control at Close-In

The closing in and drywalling of your job are critical junctures. Rough carpentry, electrical, plumbing, heating, ventilation, and air-conditioning rough-ins are complete. At this point the production manager should review the paperwork and then hold a thorough walk-through with the lead carpenter. They need to check that all rough-ins are located properly and that preparation is complete for the subsequent phases of the job.

Any problems found during this walk-through are much easier and less costly to cure than they would be after insulation and drywall is completely installed. Problems missed at this stage may not be caught until the end of the job.

A Punchlist Philosophy

You don't want your company quality to rest on "what the customer will settle for." Companies need to have their own standards, and each employee needs to work to this standard as closely as possible or exceed it. Yet, final job quality represents a mix of the remodeler's quality level and the customer's input.

Undoubtedly, you—like all successful remodelers—will also handle special punchlist items that mean a lot to the customer even though you may feel the original workmanship was adequate. For this reason, a double punchlist system is effective. After an internal punchlist is done by the lead carpenter, the customer is formally walked through the job by the production manager with the lead carpenter participating, and a final punchlist is made.

The Final Company Inspection

You don't want any punchlist. But if there has to be one, ensure that it does not become a long list of leftovers. As the job is drawing to a close, some carpenters get in the habit of saying, "We'll catch everything at the final punchlist," and let minor problems wait until then. If loose ends are handled as they arise, a minimum of work is left to do at the end when the customer is anxious to take possession of the new space.

🐾 COACHING TIP

Do you find yourself not completing punchlists quickly because you don't want to pull your carpenter off the new job and send him back? Tell that new buyer upfront that the carpenter will need a day for final touchup on his/her previous job. Tell them that you know they understand because when it comes their turn for final touchup they'll want their work done promptly too.

Near the end of the job, cut down on items to be done at the last minute by keeping a pad of paper handy on which both the customer and the lead carpenter add unfinished items. This list is worked on constantly, and items are crossed off as they are completed.

When the job is nearly done, the carpenter reviews the job totally, rereads all the paperwork, and walks slowly through the job to add any outstanding items to the list. Because each job is unique, no checklist can cover every little thing that might need attention on a job.

The sample questions listed below are just a beginning for a thorough lead carpenter's inspection:

? Is the trim properly installed and nails set?

? Is the grout cleaned from ceramic tile?

? Is the subfloor flash-patched for owner's carpet installation?

? Is the yard cleaned up and back in order?

? Has owner been given the warranty and operating instructions for all new materials and appliances?

? Are shower rods installed?

? Do all doors have stops installed?

Only when the carpenter is proud of the work and ready to have the customer and production manager review the job, should the the precompletion punchlist meeting be scheduled.

The Precompletion Punchlist

The precompletion punchlist serves three purposes:

◄ It is an agreement between the company and the customer that the resulting list of items to be completed signals the end of the job and payment of the final bill. Any items found later will be handled during the 1-year warranty period. This practice is intended to prevent customers from presenting one punchlist after another and extending final payment endlessly.

◄ It provides an opportunity for the company to review its own internal quality control.

◄ It allows the production manager and lead carpenter to sound out the customer on how well they like their design, how comfortable they were kept during construction and what suggestions the buyer would have for changes your company might make to improve.

The production manager should address all of these purposes in the walk-through with the client. If previous checks were properly done, this punchlist should be very short.

COACHING TIP

You or your production manager might want to look for at least one legitimate item to add to the punchlist that the customer did not notice. This practice shows the customer that the company is serious about its commitment to quality and service and is not relying only on the client's ability to find problems.

After the written punchlist has been developed and signed, the production manager estimates the time needed, establishes a date(s), and then schedules the subcontractors, material deliveries, and the lead carpenter all for the same time. This procedure allows you to control the timing, keeps the lead carpenter on the job to make sure no damage is done to the customer's property, and finishes the job with dispatch.

Punchlists can be handled efficiently. Taking forever to finish a punchlist—the last 2% of the job—can easily lose all the goodwill built up during the rest of the work on the job.

Handling of Warranty Problems

Every remodeler has callbacks. Some are serious; some are nuisances. It's easy to assume that the door "that sticks" can wait 3 or 4 weeks. You don't want to pull your carpenter off the ongoing job. Yet callbacks should receive priority over ongoing work in the company. Try to handle all callbacks within one week of the customer's report.

Many stationery companies and office supply firms sell three-part work order forms that are helpful in tracking callbacks. The person taking the report writes as clear a description of the problem as possible. This person may also suggest certain actions the owner can take to be sure it is a true callback. For example, if an appliance is not operating, the person receiving the call may request that the homeowner check the electrical circuit breaker. If the water pressure at a faucet seems poor, they can ask the owner to unscrew the strainer to see if flow is impeded by particles stirred up during construction.

If the call proves to be a true callback, the company person should find out what material will be needed by the carpenter or subcontractor who will return to the job. Often this information will save a later trip to a supply house and valuable worker time. An appointment is set, access to the home assured, and the callback is handled expeditiously.

The Systems Approach to Remodeling

By having these production systems in place, you have anticipated the most common stumbling blocks to a successful and profitable job and have developed specific procedures meant to head off trouble. It may be frustrating to think about the work involved in setting up and monitoring each step but it soon becomes habit and you won't know how you ever did without these trouble-preventers.

15

■ ■

Mastery

The dictionary defines **mastery** as the possession of consummate skill or as full command of some subject. Each of us strives to obtain mastery in our business. Rather than thinking of this consummate skill as a **destination,** perhaps we should focus on the **journey** that takes us there.

You've arrived at this last chapter of *Mastering the Business of Remodeling.* Are you feeling proud because what is written here corroborates what you are already doing in your company? Or are you overwhelmed because you recognize there is so much you must do? Don't be overwhelmed. Just decide the single next step you want to take and (as Nike so eloquently says) "Just do it." If you are a good businessperson, you will be improving your company until the day they lay you in your grave. There is no stopping. No destination.

Only a journey.

Mastering the Business of Remodeling

Essential Books for Today's Remodeler: The Professional Remodeler's Library

These books are designed and written to be of maximum benefit to the professional remodeler. Complete this form, or list titles, include postage (see formula at the end), enclose payment and send your order to:

Remodeling Consulting Services, Inc.
9834 Capitol View Avenue
Silver Spring, MD 20910

(301) 588-8172
FAX (301) 587-6343

Orders must be accompanied by check or money order, Visa, MasterCard, or Discover number and card expiration date. We also accept telephone and FAX orders with a Visa, MasterCard, or Discover number.

Qty.	Titles	Price	Total
____	Mastering the Business of Remodeling **NEW**	$ 35.00	_____
____	The Remodeler's Guide to Making and Managing Money	$27.00	_____
____	The Remodelers Marketing PowerPak	$ 27.00	_____
____	The Contractor's Legal Kit	$ 60.00	_____
____	Selling Remodeling: Nine Steps to Sales Success	$ 23.00	_____
____	Design/Build for Remodelers, Builders, Architects	$ 24.00	_____
		Subtotal	_____
		* Maryland residents add 5% sales tax	_____
		* Postage/Handling	$3.00

($3.00 for first book and $1.50 for each additional book)

Additional books' Postage/Handling ____ x $1.50 = _____

TOTAL ENCLOSED _____

Additional Services Offered by Remodeling Consulting Services, Inc.

BUSINESS AND MARKETING CONSULTING

Searching for Business Solutions?

- How can I achieve a thriving business and a balanced personal life?

- How can I maximize my income?

- How can I encourage all my employees to invest in my company's success?

Don't waste a minute. Call (301) 588-8172 today to schedule your **Strategic Business Analysis** with award-winning industry expert, Linda Case, or **Marketing Analysis** with RCSI Vice President, Victoria Downing.

REMODELERS EXECUTIVE ROUNDTABLES

If you own a professional remodeling company with a yearly volume of $750,000+, join Remodelers Executive Roundtables today for greater profits, a business under control, and a life that's more enjoyable. Join the other top remodelers in this exclusive group. Act today to receive more information.

REMODELERS
Executive
round tables

SEMINARS AND WORKSHOPS

If your organization is looking for innovative, informative educational programs for your members or customers, call today for information on the variety of seminars and workshops offered by nationally-known speakers, Linda Case and Victoria Downing. From *The Challenge of Success in Remodeling* to *Powerful Sales Presentations*, RCSI has the program to fit your needs.

Reader Reply Form

☑ **Please send me information on RCSI Services especially:**

☐ The Strategic Business Analysis

☐ The Marketing Analysis

☐ Remodelers Executive Roundtables, the executive think-tank for the owners of remodeling companies with volumes of $750,000+.

☐ Workshops, keynotes, and seminars.

Name _____

Company _____

Address City/State/Zip _____

Phone _____ FAX _____

Volume $_____

Send to: **Remodeling Consulting Services, Inc.**

9834 Capitol View Avenue
Silver Spring, MD 20910
(301) 588-8172
FAX (301) 587-6343
email:rcsmart1@aol.com

REMODELING
CONSULTING
SERVICES
INCORPORATED